Widow's Weeds:

Lessons Learned from the Death of a Partner

Lisa Courtney

Note for Librarians: A cataloguing record for this book is available from Library and Archives Canada at www.collectionscanada.ca/amicus/index-e.html
ISBN 1-4120-8800-3

Artwork courtesy of Lisa Courtney.

"The Same Old Sun" by Eric Woolfson and Alan Parsons from the Alan Parsons Project album *Vulture Culture*, used by permission from BMG Music Publishing.

Line from the song "You Took the Words Right Out of My Mouth (Hot Summer Night)" from the album *Bat Out of Hell* used by kind permission of Jim Steinman.

Cover photography courtesy of Patrick Riordan and cover and book design by Brenda L. Potts.

Printed in Victoria, BC, Canada. Printed on paper with minimum 30% recycled fibre. Trafford's print shop runs on "green energy" from solar, wind and other environmentally-friendly power sources.

TRAFFORD PUBLISHING™

Offices in Canada, USA, Ireland and UK

Book sales for North America and international:
Trafford Publishing, 6E–2333 Government St.,
Victoria, BC V8T 4P4 CANADA
phone 250 383 6864 (toll-free 1 888 232 4444)
fax 250 383 6804; email to orders@trafford.com
Book sales in Europe:
Trafford Publishing (UK) Limited, 9 Park End Street, 2nd Floor
Oxford, UK OX1 1HH UNITED KINGDOM
phone 44 (0)1865 722 113 (local rate 0845 230 9601)
facsimile 44 (0)1865 722 868; info.uk@trafford.com
Order online at:
trafford.com/06-0556

10 9 8 7 6 5 4 3 2

This is for Tony, of course—
whose beautiful brown eyes used to look at me
that way.

Do not stand at my grave and weep.
I am not there. I do not sleep.
I am a thousand winds that blow;
I am a diamond's glint on snow.
I am the sunlight on ripened grain;
I am the gentle autumn's rain.
When you awaken in the morning's hush,
I am the swift uplifting rush
Of quiet birds in circled flight.
I am the soft star that shines at night.
Do not stand at my grave and cry.
I am not there.
I did not die.

—Anonymous

Contents

Foreword

When Tony's hospice nurse first asked me to visit him, I was warned that he was "a charmer" and that I would need to make sure that he was kept on task. I was never exactly sure what that perceived task was (at least from the nurse's viewpoint), but as a hospice grief counselor I was ready and willing to sit with Tony as he examined the myriad questions he faced at the end of his walk upon this planet.

Entering Tony and Lisa's household for the first time, I was keenly aware of cats. I have always been a self-proclaimed "dog person" and the challenge of entering a kingdom dominated by the feline species was going to test my ability to be a clean slate for the "charmer" who sat before me. I was also a bit disconcerted that Lisa was sitting in the kitchen, ostensibly working at her computer, while Tony and I sat but a few feet away engaging in a conversation that I knew needed a sense of safety and privacy in order to be successful.

What happened in that conversation and in other conversations with Tony is not for public consumption and no one else's business. Tony's issues rest peacefully (or maybe not so peacefully) with him wherever he calls home these days. Although, if truth be told, I do so hope that he is conversing about Viking funerals and labyrinths on some cosmic level.

But the point here is that there *were* further conversations after that initial one. And may I tell you that Lisa and her computer were never again in attendance. Why?

As I remember that first day with Tony, and the energy that emanated from the kitchen, I am all too keenly aware that what was occurring was a simple act of love. If new people were going to enter Tony's life at this time, they had damned well better be ready to play the game to the fullest; Lisa was going to make sure of that. Once that was accomplished, she could be present elsewhere.

My life and work teach me that a grief response is a love response, no matter how much pain the relationship being grieved may have encompassed. And Lisa's actions that day reinforced that lesson for me. And there are other lessons here as well.

We are born with an instinctual response to loss, and that response we have called "grief." It is not something we learn, it is integral to who we are. Our culture then teaches us early on that there are "proper" ways of expressing grief, and this we have come to call "mourning." And oh, by the way, let's reserve these responses for the big events in life, not for the day-to-day moments of quiet recognition that somehow things are different and our feet are a bit less steady on the ground.

Finally, what is often overlooked is the event that precedes both grief and mourning, the fundamental building block of the human experience — change. Step back for a moment from all of the baggage that the word "grief" carries, and sit at the feet of change. If you can do that, you will learn this: All change, no matter how positive, will bring loss. And each loss will demand a grief response of some kind. Sound simple? Perhaps. But as Lisa will teach you, no one provides us with a script for working with change and the loss and grief that it brings.

Listen to the musicality of change in Lisa's stories. You will find it in the most unexpected places: in the touch of a hand, in a scratched lens, in a succession of rings, in rock and roll. She will indeed teach you that a grief response is a love response no matter how filled it is with rage or irreverence. She will show you potentials lost and potentials gained. She will point you to possibilities. And as you listen to her composition, you will learn that the change/ loss/ grief equation doesn't really end there; the ongoing spiral continues with the growth that occurs when we embrace the wisdom that grief can hold for us.

Come closer. Listen to the music. So many possibilities.

Rex Allen
Providence Hospice of Seattle

Acknowledgements

This book was not always a labor of love; sometimes it was a labor of rage, often a labor of tears, sadness and loneliness. It was also a labor of laughter, although I admit that I did most of the laughing at myself in retrospect (and at memories of Tony and me, which I didn't think I would ever do again).

I want to thank the people who made it possible for me to face the internal work I had to do, as well as the external expression of that work, which became this book:

Loving thanks to the following gentlefolk who read each chapter almost as soon as it was safely out of my system, and encouraged me to keep working on them, (and consequently on myself, too) when I was more discouraged than inspired: Elizabeth Jones, Jane Mackinnon, Kim DeWeese, Mary Margaret Feagin, Nancy Monson, Shari Wetherby and Stacey Eck each lived or re-lived parts of these stories with me. I am unimaginably blessed to have their energy shining so brightly in my life.

Thanks, too, to the rest of the Not-So-Gentle Readers, who kept me honest, questioned me when I didn't want to be questioned, and helped me to find new perspectives and a sense of peace about my processes that I couldn't have found on my own: Brenda Potts, Donna Corey, Madrona Bourdeau, Sheila Henderson, Tom Des Brisay, Tracy Doering, Steffani Stephens and Martine Hebrant made sure I did it right. I'm lucky to have them around (most of the time).

Special thanks to Jim Steinman for generously giving me permission to quote one of his most provocative and very best lines ever (I've used it in "Commuting With Meat"), and to BMG Music Publishing for granting permission to include the lyrics to Eric Woolfson and Alan Parsons' song "The Same Old Sun," which became and remains an anthem in the music track that is my life.

Tony wouldn't have wanted to be a part of this book; he would have much preferred that I'd learned my lessons through some *other* hellacious series of episodes and left him out of the picture entirely. He would have approved, though, of the notion that the sharing of our experiences could be helpful to others facing the same kinds of challenges we did. He was fond of putting a small candle in the window to help me find my way in the dark, and he's effectively done it again, albeit after the fact: the drawing that punctuates the end of each story was one that I found in one of his sketch books after he was gone.

Additional thanks to Brenda Potts for her beautiful design work and her patience, to Patrick Riordan for his creative energy and his magical eye, to Stacey Eck for her tireless assistance and good sense, to Jane Mackinnon for gracing the cover, to "The Ladies of the Book" (they know why), and to Rex Allen for writing the Foreword and thus making me look almost reputable.

Introduction

WHEN I FIRST STARTED WRITING the stories that evolved into this book, I showed some of them to a few people I know well. After reading them, one of my more practical friends asked me a good question: "Who's your audience?"

I like questions that have easy, truthful answers that don't cost me anything. "Me," I said. "I'm writing these for me."

And I was.

These stories were penned in no particular order, which, for me, reflects the fact that memories come when they come, often unbidden, sometimes unwanted, seeping into our awareness like cold winter wind under an unprotected door. They are stories of my life with and without my husband Tony, and what I seem to have learned in the process.

My darling husband Tony died of a cancer unglamorously called retroperitoneal liposarcoma in September of 2001, after having lived with, in spite of, through, and around the disease and all its related baggage for ten full years (plus one week). We were together for almost twenty-one years, which means that half of our time together was conducted within shouting distance of the menacing shadow of his illness.

After he was gone, my life spiraled aimlessly through too many dark nights I never knew existed. They were harsh and unnerving places, stark and prickly colors of sadness and fear colliding with pain-filled internal noise I realized I had been carrying for years. The only way for me to begin to make sense of and track the changes as I moved from raw pain toward something that hurt me less was to push myself back to some of the hardest episodes of Tony's illness, and force myself to remember them in detail so I could look more closely at what had happened to him/me/us. I struggled to pull a lesson, a smile or even a blessing from each memory, something that would add to the garden of life that I was trying desperately to replant and nurture in my soul.

Two years after he died, I sat down and started to write. It was the best way I knew to reconnect with myself, which was something

I had not been able to do for a long while. I started by writing only about Tony, how much I missed him and how courageous he was. After that, I wrote about how Tony could be so noble and so annoying at the same time, and in so doing, I caught myself smiling— slowly at first, then chuckling to myself, and finally laughing out loud sometimes at the strange and not-always-wonderful ways he and I tried to cope with the insidious cancer that followed us like a breathless, off-key echo.

I knew I was ready to learn to survive through my writing when I came to terms with the notion that moving forward toward healing is less about trying to live life without Tony and more about actually living life by myself, with myself, and for myself.

And somehow, *Widow's Weeds: Some Lessons Learned from the Death of a Partner* was born. As I began to limp away from "Oh God, Tony's gone, I can't breathe!" and found myself some two years down the path owning the stunned realization that "Oh God, Tony's been gone two years and I'm still breathing!" it occurred to me that if I could draw lessons from the stories of my loss, and could manage to create a space in my world for a new garden to grow, maybe someone else could benefit from what I'd learned the hard way. My goal became not so much to spare anyone else the pain of learning a lesson (we can't do that for each other too often), but to be able to extend my hand for someone else to hold on to when he or she was moving through similar territory. Maybe I could help someone else not feel as alone as I had when I went through it.

"Widow's weeds": the funeral and post-funeral black clothes worn by women whose husbands died, women in mourning. Often widows wore their weeds for the full year following the death; sometimes they wore them for the rest of their lives. Queen Victoria wore her widow's weeds for her beloved Prince Albert for the rest of her life, an outward expression of her terrible grief and loss that became a cultural standard for the statement and ready recognition of grief. The wearing of widow's weeds was a societal expectation in nineteenth-century society that still has a tenuous hold on us today.

I think about widow's weeds in a different way. In my own case, widow's weeds are the things that grow in the flowering orchard that is my soul. Contained there are the fragrant and lovely buds and blossoms as well as the thistled, sharp and too-deeply-rooted plants of perhaps somewhat dubious origin. But they all grow in the same soil—mine. I own and tend it all.

One person's flowers are another person's weeds: this is doubly true for me since I have come to view most everything that grows in my soul as worthy of sunlight; every bit of green growth matters and is cherished for itself in the moment. Yesterday's favorite flower, whatever its shape and scent, may not be the choice of my heart today.

My widow's weeds are lessons and choices, too, prompted by memory, pain, loss, stubbornness, grief, laughter and loneliness. My weeds grow freely; they fill a scatter garden of color, texture and an uncommon but somehow acceptable lack of design. Not only do my roses have thorns, they exhale sounds. My crabgrass carries the smell of fresh calmness even as it fights daily to dominate other flora I might prefer to have grow in its place. There are dandelions everywhere, don't ask why. My garden is sometimes an herb farm, other times an orchard. It's a rockery, a dangerous swamp, a rose-covered trellis, a sacred arbor and a jungle. Most often, it's a startling combination of all of these things.

Take a quiet stroll along the path through the now-steady ground where I grow my widow's weeds; meet Tony and me, and walk with us. And if something interests you along the way, stop and look at it, experience its sweetness or taste its bitterness, laugh at whatever amuses you, cry if you feel like it. Flow with the energy you find here, and take from it whatever you need.

Warning: You should not read this book if:

You prefer to deal with death, loss and grief solely in traditional, comfortable ways; or

You are uncomfortable talking about or hearing about death; or

You have ever stood in line for the opportunity to be deeply offended by something (I am glib to the point of being very close to downright rude); or

You have certain expectations about how death should be appropriately, acceptably articulated (or you don't think that issues about death, especially *personal* ones, should be articulated at all); or

You don't know how to or don't want to see the potential for laughter, especially where illness, death, and life are concerned; or

You just don't want to go there (I can and do respect that).

Don't worry, I won't be offended if you don't want to read this book. I didn't tell these stories for you, after all. I wrote them for me. See? I told you the truth in the first place.

But if I can help, by showing you that you're not entirely alone in a paradigm that threatens to drown you, if I can point to one more possible road out of the darkness and go with you to a place where I have seen a little light, then go ahead and read this book. It might be exactly what you need right now.

I am sorry for your loss, truly sorry. And I'm sorry for mine. Let's talk about where we go from here.

Lisa Courtney

March 2006

"I should sculpt your face," you said.
I was twenty-four and adorable
and in my frenetic youth could no more sit still for you
than I could fly.
You were busy with other things too
so there is no sculptural form
of Lisa at twenty-four.

"Why haven't I sculpted your face?" you asked.
I was thirty-six and finally exchanging girlhood for true womanhood,
finding my way through uncomfortable mazes of my own design,
perpetually in motion, no time for sitting still for you,
dreaming of flying.
And you were busy with other things too
planning journeys of your own
so there is no sculptural form
of Lisa at thirty-six.

"I should have sculpted your face," you whispered.
I am forty-three now and am the best and brightest form of myself so far.
And while I can finally sit still for you
(should you choose to commit my image to clay at last)
today I realize this:

you have indeed sculpted my face, every day we have lived together;
    the laugh lines around my eyes were lovingly placed there by your own sweet and funny soul
    the depth and width of my smile comes from years of genuine delight at being with you
and the desire that shapes my mouth was crafted by two decades of kisses and conversation.

My face is my own
and somehow
because you have touched it with magic and mischief in mind
it is yours, too.
You have shared in the sculpting of it
with all the love you have held in your gentle, sculptor's hands;
I can see and feel the touches of your masterful work whenever I pass a mirror or a window
    —the bright light and playful shadow that you brought into my life
and then slowly added to the hungry landscape of my face—
and now
I bless you for your subtle art
each and every time I fly.

for Tony
May 1, 2000

The Wilkinsons

MR. AND MRS. WILKINSON, OUR neighbors, were the first adults I ever saw holding hands.

They lived in the big house that stood catty-cornered on the other side of the street from the one I grew up in, at the very end of the block. I never got a good look at the outside of their house; it was surrounded by a tall, thick and silently intimidating hedge that bordered their corner property. The neighborhood children stayed outside of that border as if by tacit understanding; we didn't even stop there for candy at Halloween.

The Wilkinsons didn't have kids (that we knew of), which was, of course, unheard of during our Late-Baby-Boomer childhood. If they weren't providing us with additional playmates, there was no reason to pay that much attention to them, and most of the time, we didn't.

They kept to themselves. Even the adult neighbors, whose child-filled homes were in much closer proximity to the Wilkinson's than my parents' home was, didn't know them beyond a polite wave when passing in cars or on foot. While never openly snubbed or entirely ostracized, they were quietly considered *The Odd Ones* in our mostly middle-class suburban community, and were left alone, not invited to block parties or other neighborhood activities.

And we were kids, caught up in our own busy little worlds. We had no reason to think twice about grownups in general; Mr. and Mrs. Wilkinson were not among the adults we normally had to deal with, so we ignored them as a matter of course. We knew them on sight, and that was enough for us. There was no reason to think about them.

At least, I didn't think about them, not once, for more than thirty years. Inexplicably, one day I found myself remembering them, not long after Tony died.

I never knew much of anything about them. The Wilkinsons were German, and middle-aged (which of course read as *ancient* to me when I was nine or ten). They were both a little chubby; there was a sense of geometric balance to the subtle solidity of them.

Mr. Wilkinson was a cheerful man, and his face was always a little flushed. He wore a green hat in fall and winter that had a small feather in it. He had a ready, wide smile for us kids when we scurried past him, but it seems to me now that the smile was one always directed at his wife. When he looked at her, his eyes glittered.

Mrs. Wilkinson had long hair, a deep shade of cinnamon brown that was darker in my early childhood, and took on silvery streaks as I grew older. She always wore her hair in a tight, neat bun, every hair in place despite the walk, regardless of the weather. She wore a camel-colored beret on the days when her husband wore his hat.

The Wilkinsons walked briskly around the block close to every single weekday of my childhood. They passed my house like clockwork, around four in the afternoon; it didn't matter if the day was rain-streaked and windy, or bitingly cold and snowy, or sunny and mild, or blisteringly humid. They moved easily around and through a score of noisy, active neighborhood children, and down the big hill that crested at the foot of my parent's driveway.

And as they walked, they held hands.

My parents didn't hold hands. I own not a single memory of my mother touching my father at all, except for the routine off-to-work and home-from-work pecks they gave each other. I know they must have danced on occasion (and therefore had to be touching at some point), and I have several siblings, so there was some touching going on there, too. The point is that my parents didn't touch each other in front of their children; there was no easy, affectionate hand-holding going on in my home.

Not so for The Wilkinsons. Each day, as they took their afternoon walk, they held hands, talking quietly with each other. He smiled at her, she chuckled and gave him a look in return that I had never seen before, and wouldn't see for another dozen years or so, when I'd catch Tony looking exactly that way at me.

I never actually spoke to either of them, apart from a polite, mostly meaningless hello; I was a kid who had no genuine interest in the adults who already over-peopled my world, and I wasn't looking to take any more of them on.

But all these years later, I remember them walking down the

hill on the pavement across the street from my house. They were holding hands, absolutely in love (I can see that now, didn't pay attention to it then), taking in the fresh air and talking contentedly together in a way that I couldn't have understood at the time, talking intimately, with a closeness that seemed so foreign to what I saw in my parents.

But that's not what I meant to tell you.

What I meant to tell you is that I really miss holding hands with Tony.

We held hands much of the time; when we went for walks, while riding in the car, when we watched TV together, when we made love. Sometimes we held hands over dinner, even after we'd been married for nearly twenty years. Touching each other, just holding each other's hand, was grounding and centering and happy for both of us. When we talked about important things, we always held hands. I can only recall two specific conversations in the two decades of our marriage that occurred without the safety of my fingers cradled comfortably in his.

I can close my eyes and still feel the touch of his strong thumb moving gently across the knuckles on the back of my hand.

After he was gone, the sight of couples kissing, or embracing each other, didn't bother me at all. I was glad for them.

What filled my eyes with sad and hungry tears, a thing that fed a constantly-renewing sense of unspeakable loss, was the unbidden sight of couples holding hands as they walked ahead of me toward a movie theater, or when they laced their fingers together as they ate dinner in a restaurant at the table immediately next to mine.

When I saw older couples holding hands with the precious, casual familiarity that I would never have with Tony again, I had to look away; my misery was uncontained fire and there were never tears enough to put it out.

It took me almost two years to be able to stand quietly and watch other hands being held without my heart ripping into tight, jagged shards of pain.

Practice makes perfect: I barely notice it now, and have taught myself not to feel it. At least, not very much.

I do not know what ultimately happened to the Wilkinsons. I packed up my little life and left for the West Coast to go to college two months after I graduated from high school, and rarely returned to my parents' Philadelphia home.

I never gave the Wilkinsons a second thought.

I've been thinking about them recently, though.

I will never ask my mother what happened to them in the end. I do not want to know which of them died first, and if the surviving Wilkinson continued to walk, sad and alone now, around the block every day, with a longing, empty hand crammed agonizingly into a coat pocket because it had no where else to go.

I don't want to think about it.

But I've been thinking about it a great deal, of course. There's no one here any longer to hold my hand, and I can't squeeze a message back into the warm and loving fingers of the man who knew me so well. I feel that part of my loss keenly.

And yet perhaps the salvation, my salvation, is this: as heavy as my own sorrow is at times, I can think about The Wilkinsons, remember them walking in my memory, and see them holding hands forever. When I allow myself to step out of the dark circle of my solitary despair, and genuinely appreciate and understand the quiet comfort they found in each other, I can feel a different, separate shade of pain, pain for *them*, at the thought of the terrible loss that one of them must have suffered. When my focus is pulled slightly away from myself, and I consider the feelings of someone else, I find it is easier for me to move a few halting steps out of the darkness of my blinding grief and slowly navigate my way toward a warm and welcoming ray of the waiting, healing light.

Scratched Lenses

WHEN TONY AND I WERE in Scotland the year before he died, he fell hard over a curb in Edinburgh. He went down like a prizefighter, hit his knee and his left cheek on the pavement, and scratched the heavy left lens in his glasses.

Believe it or not, it's kind of a happy memory for me. Once I got over being frightened out of my wits by the suddenness and helplessness of the fall, and once I was certain that (all things considered) he was mostly all right, we continued on to the gallery we were headed for, and had a good rest of the day.

Later, back in our hotel room, we got specific about inspecting the damage. He had a bruise and bad scrape on his cheek, a deep gouge in his glasses lens, and his knee was shredded and bruised, and would ultimately take a month to heal.

We then disintegrated into a heated argument about his somewhat surly perceptions of my (in)ability to offer general first aid. He frowned at my attempts to get his cheek and his knee cleaned up, disinfected, and bandaged appropriately.

He didn't feel great; the fall had made him hurt all over. Cranky now, he was up for a fight. "You," he said, pointing at me with an accusing finger, "are a terrible nurse."

"Nice talk for the one who's going to be stuck taking care of you later," I scowled at him.

"I can't believe I never knew how useless you are at dealing with stuff like this," Tony snapped, grabbing the antiseptic wipe from my hand and dabbing at his knee with it in a motion only slightly different from the one I'd been using a moment before. "How can you not know basic first aid?" he asked, incredulous. "At your age!"

Frustrated but articulate as ever, I gestured fiercely at him. When the message was duly received, he glared at me and I left the room in a huff, punctuating my irritation with a sharp slam of the door.

It was not the first time I'd wondered vaguely how I was going to take care of Tony when his illness was the loudest music in our life together. But it was the first time I wondered if I could actually *do* it, take on the responsibility of the constant care, on all the levels that would be required of me. And the doubt he'd suddenly opened up in me stealthily and silently haunted me for a long time after that.

A part of me hated him for it, and that scared me. Jarred by the intensity of my negative feelings, I hurriedly buried them, and went for a long walk.

We made up, of course, as soon as I strolled calmly back into the hotel room an hour or so later. We could never stay angry with each other for long; we were laughing before I managed to get the door to our room closed. Laughter was woven deeply into the fabric of our relationship; we were happy together, despite occasional lapses, and we could always crack each other up, no matter what.

Not even cancer could alter that.

But that's not what I meant to tell you.

What I meant to tell you is that, when we came home after the trip, we never replaced the badly-scratched lens in Tony's glasses. There are some odd reasons: he didn't complain about it, and so I let myself overlook and then forget about it; it didn't seem to impair his vision much (although when I think back on it now, it probably did); the glasses were terribly expensive at a time when we were looking into alternative cancer treatments not covered by insurance; and we'd spent a lot of money in Scotland. Most of all, it didn't make sense to me, although I never spoke the words to him, to spend considerable cash to replace a costly lens for someone who was most likely not going to be alive long enough to get our money's worth out of the transaction.

I let myself forget about the scratched lens.

After Tony was gone and I slowly started going through his things, deciding what to keep and what to sadly let go of, I found myself running my fingers over the deep and now troubling scratch in the lens in his glasses before I placed them lovingly beside his wedding ring in my jewelry box.

He had lived a full year past the Scotland trip, despite his doctors' predictions and assessments to the contrary. He had uncomplainingly tolerated the scratched lens for the rest of his life.

I tell myself earnestly that if I had believed then that he would have been with me for another whole year, I would have had that lens replaced immediately upon our return home. And I would have, surely.

I think.

It's possible that the bitterness I carried about the life that Tony's cancer was stealing from him, and from me, too, got in my way. It's possible that in a small but petty, vicious way I was subconsciously smacking him for being the unwilling vehicle through which cancer was killing him and destroying me. That scratched lens is one of the few things that I ever left unresolved when it came to doing anything for or taking care of Tony, and for that reason alone I question my motives, my feelings, and my shaky sense of my own innocence.

The scratched lens doesn't accuse me. It simply invites me to notice, and, by noticing, to think and to learn.

Not long ago, I had dinner out with a friend. At the end of the meal, I reached for my glasses, and found that they had fallen from the table. I retrieved them from the floor by my feet; I had stepped on them.

Upon examination, I discovered a long, thin scratch across the left lens. Although I tried, the scratch wouldn't rub out. When I wear them, I can see well enough, but the truth is that the lens needs to be replaced.

I'll get around to it one of these days. Or maybe not.

The Midnight Run

LAST NIGHT I HAD TO make a Midnight Run to the emergency vet with three-year-old Duncan, my precious flame-point Siamese. He's fine, now, nothing to worry about. It isn't the fact that he was unwell and in pain that is on my mind this morning, or the fact that the emergency vet is of necessity so much more expensive than my regular vet during normal business hours. I am not flustered that I have to alter poor Duncan's diet to regulate the amount of pH in his food intake to keep him from having further problems.

For a while, until Duncan is content with his dietary changes, or at least resigned to them, I'm going to have to do some careful juggling to keep things in my small feline community sane and somehow balanced. I don't want Duncan's dietary restrictions to be a bigger stomachache than they need to be, for any of us. Jasmine is nearly eighteen years old and only eats "junk" cat food, and that's her right and privilege. Fiona, at ten, prefers the "junk" food but I'm going to work to coax her into eating the prescription food Duncan has to eat now. She's pretty amenable most of the time, but this eating thing is going to be something of a challenge for all of us.

Naturally, that's exactly what I *don't* want in my life…uneasy challenges and more juggling.

In the cold reality of dealing with Tony's cancer, I felt like I was forever dancing, dangerously barefooted, on the edges of dozens of razor blades, sharp or dull or thin or wide. I hate that I know how to do it now, but I don't fight it as much or perhaps as hard as I used to. And that counts for some sort of growth, doesn't it?

In the last months of Tony's life, I became a master at juggling while dancing fast. I handled all of the spontaneous alterations of his heavy drug regimen, all the while doing a little soft-shoe of the soul. I waltzed around and coordinated visits from friends to keep him occupied and entertained but not overwhelmed. I learned more about his illness and general care-giving than I ever wanted to know, to the beat of a tango which kept time by the uneasy pounding of my heart. I twisted the nights away keeping doctors and hospice nurses apprised of the day's events. I moved our life through its own small marriage ballet according to Tony's moods, his varying energy levels and ever-changing needs: I made sure he rested; I nagged at him to keep his feet up to stave off the edema for one more day; I cajoled him into eating…the list now seems endless to me, and makes me tired just thinking about it. It's enough to say I juggled hard and danced with almost manic precision, tripping the light horrific. I didn't (or I *couldn't*) stop the constant, frenetic movement until there was, finally, no reason to continue.

It didn't occur to me until I sped down the freeway in the dark last night with Duncan in the carrier beside me that I was doing it all over again. Here I was, racing to the Emergency Room, making the dreaded and all-too-familiar Midnight Run.

I had forgotten about the stress and its underlying sense of hopelessness. I don't think I even articulated this to myself last night; I only felt the feelings, and remembered. That was enough to shake me.

I admit that the Midnight Run was definitely in the top five things I hated most about the entire experience of effectively playing the capable wife of a man who was living with cancer. I knew the eighteen long miles from our driveway to the front door of the ER with a brittle, icy intimacy. I knew how to chatter lightly and incessantly during the Run to keep us both faintly occupied so neither of us would be entirely afraid and miserable about the next new development (or the sorry rehashing of an old one) that the ER staff would hopefully be able to ease. I knew how to stay just glib enough with him so that I could maintain a decent pretense of an internal balance I could not own or touch or feel, and appear to be in control (ha) of getting us where we needed to go so we could do the next thing.

Yes, I'd all but forgotten about the Midnight Run…until last night with Duncan.

They've all come flooding back, now, the tension-filled memories enveloping me, threatening me with far more than a random sip at the well; today it would be so easy to simply let myself drown in the sadness and despair of it all. I wouldn't have to fight; I'd only have to fall a short distance and allow the dark waters in.

But that would get me nowhere.

I don't like remembering the many hellish episodes of The Midnight Run. But I can summon any one of them at will. Sometimes they come of their own accord, and all I can do is wait for the scenes to pass and leave me alone.

And here I go again, thinking and rehashing, against my better judgment. In each Run there was a constant ripple of unarticulated fear, the anticipation of pain far more than the hope of the relief of it, the fevered exhaustion of spirit that I had never dreamed possible. Would he be sick in the car? Was there enough gas in the tank to get us to the hospital? (I tried but often failed to keep the tank consistently at least half-full. It gave him something to cheerfully nag me about.) Would the ER staff be able to help him this time? Would they admit him and take over the majority of the caregiving for a couple of days, or would they have me take him back home after six or seven stressful hours, where he'd be my (beloved yet terrifying) responsibility again?

The Midnight Run was the flashpoint of so many smaller fires in my heart and head that of course last night's unexpected reminder with the cat makes me feel edgy and unsettled. And that's because I'm remembering that there was something else, then, too, infusing the already unhappy situation with an additional burden: my private unspoken, unspeakable anger at the heart of it all, mingling with an unholy bitterness that we had to make the Run to the hospital in the first place.

Hardest of all to take is the truth I held burning in my hands then, and that I still carry sadly in my heart: the sharp, shattering awareness that all the love in the world didn't stand a chance against the battle we were fighting.

But that's not what I meant to tell you.

What I meant to tell you is that Tony used to say (to my utter annoyance, at the most frustratingly appropriate moments): "Fair is fiction." I didn't want to believe him about this, never wanted him to be right. But he was.

The concept of "fairness" *is* fiction; there's no such thing as "fair."

We've been lied to, again; there's not always going to be a saving light at the end of the long, dark, cold tunnel. And the sun will come out tomorrow, Annie, but it may burn you to death, or maybe only blind you this time. So stop singing so hopefully, and wipe that naïve smile off of your face. I don't want to see it; I have no use for it. No one can promise you that everything will be all right, no matter how much they want to help you and no matter how much you need to believe them.

No. I've found that things are what they are, for good, or for ill. It's both very simple and very complex to get your head around. I try not to think about it, since it annoys me, but I find myself meditating upon it often.

Perhaps the best we can do is to learn to accept what comes to us, deal with it as we will, and do our best to keep on dancing.

Melissa

NINE MONTHS BEFORE TONY DIED, he met Melissa.

Melissa was and is married to a friend of mine, Jason, who'd been my boss for a short but fun period of time. It was just after Christmas 2000, and Jason wanted to take me (and Tony, too) out for dinner at one of Jason's favorite restaurants. We had never met Jason's wife before, but we looked forward to doing so and I especially liked the idea of having an extravagant dinner out, on Jason.

Tony and I arrived at the restaurant and met up with Jason and Melissa. Jason and I sat across from each other in the roomy booth, with our respective spouses beside us, also facing each other.

Dinner was wonderful; the food was fabulous and the conversation was light and casual. Jason and I talked a little shop, and eventually noticed that Melissa and Tony had not only hit it off, but were almost completely oblivious to us. They talked about art and film and theater, all topics in which Tony was more than fluent. Jason and I laughed about the spontaneous friendship bursting between our Significant Others.

I have rarely seen personal chemistry flash and spark as swiftly as Melissa's and Tony's did; I could almost hear the click of their connection. She was twenty-four, he was fifty-nine and on the tail end of his life journey; before dessert arrived, they were fast friends.

We spent about three hours together that first evening. The four of us talked easily as a group, and it was clear that Tony and I would be seeing a lot of Melissa in the coming year. By the time we had our coats on, the two of them had already made plans to get together almost immediately. Melissa was an art student, and Tony had taught art on the university level decades before; they decided that Tony would mentor Melissa twice a week, on the two days she wasn't in school. Jason and I applauded the decision; he was eager for Melissa to find her path, and was supportive of whatever she chose to do.

For my part, I was delighted by the sparkle that had crept back into Tony's eyes; it had been missing for months. I hid my amazement as I chatted casually with Jason, my heart lighter as I covertly watched my husband reanimate while he talked with

Melissa. It was so good to see him genuinely interested and engaged in something; for far too long, he had been listless and frustrated, struggling with his inability to contribute (he thought) in ways that mattered to him. He was often tired and felt understandably unwell; we had known for a long while that his cancer was inoperable, and we'd been altering our world according to what he could and couldn't do physically. I had been at a loss to find new and subtle ways of keeping him emotionally and intellectually stimulated.

Melissa was the right answer at the best time.

She came to the house on Tuesday and Thursday afternoons. I worked all week long, and could only give Tony my evenings and weekends. She was good company for him; she was smart and independent, young and pretty, and knew that she had a lot to learn about art. She also accurately gauged that Tony would and could download his wisdom, experience, creativity and perspective. She needed what he could give her, and he very much needed to give it to her.

"She's *you*," he told me one night, several weeks later. "You," he laughed merrily, "without the *taint*."

I had to stop and think about it. What was he thinking? *Could* she be me? Did he really see her that way? The more I thought about it, the more I realized that he was on to something. She and I are similarly wired in some fundamental ways. We are both outspoken, independent, articulate, analytical, intelligent and creative women. We do not tolerate stupidity; we move through life largely unafraid of the lions, tigers, and bears that lurk around dark corners. When something has to be said, we say it. (Sometimes we say it whether it needs saying or not.) We are often both strong and fearless. We are forces to be reckoned with.

So in a way, Melissa *is* me, a prettier, younger, less jaded, less tired and perhaps less experienced version of me. Once I'd been as hungry as she was for new experiences and new information that fed into my sparkling creative life; Tony had fed me well in the early days of our relationship. Over the years, as Tony's cancer became part of the subtext of our life together, there was little room for the demands of my creative energy and my need for the solitude that gave me space to write. His illness pushed much of the energy of my artistic life out of focus, and I had resigned myself to that with as little bitterness as possible. As bravely as I could, I consciously wrapped my need to create in soft sheets of wistfulness and dutifully packed them away in what I thought was a safe place, to be revisited at some point when my life made more sense. Tony hated that I'd given it up; he made best efforts to goad me into spending time with the keyboard, but my heart wasn't in it. Cancer, or the constant awareness of it, had crept into every corner of my world, and would never let go. Understanding this, I kept myself separate from my need to write for the better part of ten years, with only a few exceptions. And I kept my misery over that loss to myself.

On the other hand, Melissa had had no reason to push her creativity aside; she wore it like a glowing talisman. Tony thrived on that kind of brightness.

After some quiet consideration, I had to admit to myself that Tony was right: Melissa was, in a strange but not uncomfortable way, me. Me, before Tony's illness had crashed the party.

They talked on the phone for hours at a stretch in the early days of their friendship, their conversations sometimes creeping into the evenings and weekends that belonged to me. I could have taken exception to the interference, but rarely did. However, as is my way, when I had had enough of waiting for him to get off the phone, I told him so, and he quickly ended the conversation and gave me his attention.

I got to know Melissa better as time passed. She was usually still at the house when I came home from work on those Tuesdays and Thursdays. At the office, Jason and I joked that we were nothing more than the information transfer center between our partners.

Melissa and Tony grew closer. They talked about far more than art and jewelry and sculpture; they talked about life and politics and anything else that intrigued them at the moment. Such is the best energy behind good mentoring: he poured out his thoughts, his experience, his memories, his art, his entire world for her, and she drank it up.

He loved talking with her; he had someone new to tell his tired old stories to! I had heard—and often starred in—his stories dozens of times, and so wasn't his best audience. It was all fresh for Melissa, and Tony cheerfully unearthed a hundred stories to entertain and teach her. In giving Melissa all the things he could, he found that he was more connected with life, and better in tune with his inner self, than he'd allowed himself to be in ten years. He was doing something that mattered deeply to him; he had always loved teaching, and now he was doing it with a passion, a commitment, and a joy that made my heart sing.

Melissa, and her hunger for what was in his head, was doing more to nourish and nurture Tony's waning quality of life than anyone else in his world. Including me.

Nearly everyone who was involved in our daily rhythms got to know Melissa; she became a solid fact of Tony's life. Some of our friends questioned me about the relationship: Was there something going on between them? Was I feeling threatened? Was I harboring unspoken feelings of resentment toward her? How could I stand the thought that while I was working hard at the office, she and Tony were at home alone?

I smiled then, much as I'm smiling as I think about it now. Was Tony in love with Melissa? I believe that he was, softly and secretively; if he recognized it, he never told me about it. He did not love her in the same way he was in love with me, but I know that he loved her; he cared deeply, and reveled in her company, her humor, her brains, and her drive to open herself up fully to her creative energy. He was never once bored with her; he always looked forward to spending time with her.

Did Melissa love Tony? There's not a single doubt in my mind about that. Of course she loved him.

And I'll always be glad about that.

The year rolled by, and as spring moved into summer of 2001, Tony visibly began to slow down. Even after we initiated hospice at home, Melissa was still there on Tuesdays and Thursdays, hanging out with Tony, showing him her drawings, working on sculptural forms, talking about her jewelry class, sharing and learning.

When Tony began to have difficulty walking, fell down a few times, and began to sleep more during the day, I reminded Melissa that she really didn't have to keep coming to the house to deal with what was left of her mentor. When his body started failing in altogether new and unexpected ways, I suggested that it was unfair for her to have to cope with Tony's losing battle. I tried to let her off the hook gently. I had been concerned that as Tony neared the end of his life, it would be too much for Melissa to handle, and I wanted to spare her the horrors and the heartache of it, protect her from what I myself could not be protected from.

I didn't know then what she was made of, the young woman who was "me without the taint." She chose to continue coming to the house every Tuesday and Thursday, to learn whatever she could from him, to take whatever he was able to offer her. And she gave back, every time she was there. While she and Tony interacted during their time together, she subtly enforced my rules about making sure he rested, ate, and drank plenty of water. She quietly kept an eye on his medication, energy levels, and motor skills, and checked in with me when she noticed something going on with him that didn't feel right to her or something she didn't understand.

She also became an extremely efficient spy for me. As I drove home from work on Tuesdays and Thursdays, I'd call her and she'd let me know what he was up to. She deftly distracted him away from hazards (he was itching to play with his power tools and had not come to terms with the sorry fact that he no longer had the strength to handle them safely), and moved him toward things he could still physically manage. On more than one occasion she got him to stop doing something that would have proven to be too much for him by telling him truthfully that she had just gotten off the phone with me, I was five minutes from home, and if he got caught doing something he shouldn't be doing, she knew I was going to throttle him. She kept him safe without embarrassing him; she watched over him with a kindness and good humor that left plenty of room for him to continue to teach her, listen to her, and share his knowledge and wisdom.

Early that autumn, when I came home from work, I'd often find her sitting in the living room, curled up in a chair doing homework or reading, keeping half an eye on Tony, who was asleep on the couch. She'd tell me about their time together that day, how much he'd eaten or rested, what Roberta, our primary hospice nurse, had said (even though Roberta had already called me earlier in the day), which of our friends had stopped by to see Tony, and how those visits had gone. It occurred to me then that I was probably talking with Melissa as much as Tony himself was at that time.

He had a bad week, followed by another. The hospice nurses were coming by more often; I was on the phone with them sometimes more than once each night. He was less talkative, had less energy, but stubbornly insisted on continuing to do as much as he could. On a Tuesday in late September, he struggled to keep things easy and light as he and Melissa worked on a clay sculpture. He didn't have a lot of strength left in his arms and hands; Melissa knew it, and kept him busy, distracted, occupied and cheerful.

The following Thursday, Melissa and Tony did more talking than working, but it was the best day he'd had in what felt to me like a long time. He was tired that day, though, and napped part of the time she was there. When I got home from work, she and I had a cup of tea together, and chatted quietly as he slept. I don't even remember if he woke up before she left that evening, but I'll bet Melissa does. It was the last time she saw him.

The next day, Friday, was Tony's worst day yet; his body was painfully rebelling and he was powerless to do anything but let it happen. Hospice nurses spent much of Friday, Saturday and Sunday with us. The fight was almost over. We were losing.

Monday afternoon he went into a coma, and was gone by Tuesday morning at four a.m.

It makes me smile to realize that Tony shared his last good day with Melissa. I've tried to be jealous about that, but can't quite get the grin off of my face. She was the best thing that happened to him during that last year of his life. How could I begrudge him—or her—that last good day?

But that's not what I meant to tell you.

What I meant to tell you is that one of the hardest things I have ever had to hear had to do with Melissa, through no fault of her own.

After Tony had been gone for a few weeks, a friend of his told me something I really didn't want to know:

"Tony told me that he was so happy with Melissa around. He said that Melissa's presence reminded him constantly that he was still alive; he said that your presence reminded him constantly that he was dying."

Ouch.

This is not something that a still-hot-to-the-touch, grieving, tired, and frightened widow (who has not exactly been the very soul of effective and efficient long-term caregiving) should ever have to hear. But I heard it, and I had no choice but to own it.

As painful as it was, what he said resonates a truth I wish I didn't have to acknowledge, but acknowledge it I do.

Melissa happily participated in Tony's life, and her consistent, familiar, and welcome presence kept him actively involved in the business of living. He had information to impart (his favorite thing!), stories to tell, dreams to unfold, wisdom to offer, opinions to generate thought, guidance to lend. I believe he was more emotionally, intellectually, and creatively intimate with Melissa that last year, certainly in the last six months, than he was with me during the same period.

My job was the terrible, tedious, and frustrating one: it fell to me to hand him his dozens of pills twice a day, to translate doctor's and nurses' orders into manageable reality, to live all my days and nights with one eye on him at all times (or to coordinate the eyes that were on him in my absence), to alternately plead with him or bully him to do what needed to be done in order to keep him relatively pain-free and out of immediate danger on a daily basis. I'm the one who took the blame for the loss of each small piece of his life, each individual task that was ultimately taken away from him. He was extremely angry with me when he no longer had the physical ability to bend down and empty the cat litter boxes (the doctor insisted that I relieve him of that chore). He refused to speak to me for a full day over it, and held the notion firmly in his mind that I was trying to control him and take away his sense of usefulness. He hurled his frustration at me; there was nowhere else for him to throw it.

I was the one who had to ask "How are you?" and "Are you all right?" and "What's going on with you right now?" Of *course* I was an unwitting, constant reminder to him that he was dying.

Still, the words stung me, even when I thought them through, understood and accepted the truth of them.

One night over dinner, I told Melissa about what Tony's friend had said. Instead of denying it or trying to sidestep it, she nodded slowly and looked me in the eye. "I can see where he might have felt that way," she said grimly. "But the bottom line, what's important, is that he knew that you had to do that stuff, and he understood how much you didn't want to be the one who had to do it, and he loved you for it. He always talked about you, all the time, how much he loved you, and how he didn't want to leave you." I knew all these things without her having to tell me; just the same, though, I loved her for saying them.

Melissa became one of my closest friends. We shared Tony for a year, and then we shared our grief at the loss of him. We also shared an understanding of where we'd been together, each of us standing on either side of the man we both loved in our unique ways, quietly balancing and steadying him as he faced the end of his journey.

Melissa and I talk about Tony once in a while, but our friendship and sisterhood has less to do with him and more to do with us, which is, I think, as it should be.

He'd be so proud of her, though, delighted with how far she's come, pleased with the dreams she's opened wide and brought fully into the light. He would be entirely appreciative of the style, skill and artistry that is simply Melissa. I can see glimpses of Tony and his subtle touches in the way she approaches her life and work when I look at her, when she tells me what she's up to this month. I'm very proud of her, too, and I respect the woman she's chosen to become.

Here's the best thing: when Melissa smiles, confident as she moves along her chosen path, I can hear Tony laughing.

Lynn Caine

I KNEW VAGUELY WHO LYNN Caine was before I was in my twenties. In the event that you don't know yet, she was a woman who suffered the loss of her husband to cancer in the early 1970s, and she wrote a courageous, groundbreaking book called *Widow* that chronicled her experience. The difference between Lynn's book and anything that had hit the market before it was that Lynn had the guts and the conviction to tell it like it was.

No one was talking intimately and candidly about death in those days, although Dr. Elisabeth Kubler-Ross was addressing the issues of death and dying from an entirely different, more clinical perspective. As a society, we weren't eager to acknowledge, much less hear about, the personal side of the death of a loved one. We liked the idea that if we didn't talk about it, we wouldn't have to deal with it. And naturally it was too much of a downer for prime-time television, so we were safe from having to give death much thought. That is, until Lynn came along.

Lynn's book helped people to look at the day-to-day, personal, and sometimes intimate dynamics of loss.

After she wrote *Widow* her world opened up in ways she never expected. She spent much of her time speaking at women's conferences and appearing on television. I saw her interviewed by Barbara Walters on a program called *Not For Women Only*, where she spoke honestly and openly about the death of her husband. In telling her story, Lynn showed us that sad, difficult, grossly unfair and paralyzing things can and do happen, that we are shaped and reshaped by them, but we can survive them.

I can't tell you why I read Lynn's book as soon as it hit the bookstores when I was in my teens, but I did. I was as amazed by her candor as I was humbled by her willingness to use her own painful experiences to help others. (*Other* others, not me. I didn't need Lynn Caine, of course.)

Yeah, I knew who Lynn Caine was. But she remained a small, stray factoid in the back of my head throughout my twenties and into my thirties. I didn't have a specific reason to think about her, so I didn't. Once Tony's cancer was diagnosed, I didn't have room for anything on my mind except getting through whatever was raining on us on any particular day.

And then, about three years before Tony died, I briefly saw a counselor with whom I was working to get a handle on some of the things I was unhappily learning first-hand about terminal illness and losing a spouse. This very forward-thinking woman made a suggestion that I found disquieting: she said I should go to a bookstore, buy a couple of books about widows and widowhood, and put them away, to be read after Tony had died. She told me she had a good idea that I wouldn't be interested in buying them after the fact.

I'll admit that I thought this was just a little weird at the time, but still I was open to anything I could get my head around. I told her that I'd look into it.

Sure enough, several weeks after she suggested it, I was in a bookstore, and happened upon the self-help section, which I usually sailed past with a smirk as I made my normal stroll toward Fiction and Literature. This time I stopped, looked around, and saw a couple of books whose titles intrigued me. One was written by an author whose name I recognized in a flash: Lynn Caine. The book was called *A Compassionate, Practical Guide to Being a Widow.*

I took it home, stuck it in a drawer in one of the cabinets in my office, and I promptly forgot about it, probably in self-defense. I was not ready to read it, and told myself that I did not have the need (yet) so I didn't want to know what was in it.

The book sat undisturbed in its hiding place for more than three years. If in the normal course of rummaging through the drawer I accidentally noticed it sitting there waiting patiently for me, I moved past it quickly and actively overlooked it. I didn't tell anyone, especially Tony, that I had the book stashed away for *later*.

I dug Lynn's book out a week after Tony died.

I did not open it. I took it to the bedroom and dropped it on the dresser, where it sat for a few days.

Then it took up residence on the nightstand on his side of the bed for another week or so.

In the early days without him, I was staggeringly uncommunicative, which scared me but I couldn't seem to do anything about it. I had measurable difficulty holding three thoughts together. Most distressing of all to me was the fact that I was constantly frustrated by my inability to cope with Tony's actual passing, a situation I'd had ten solid years to consider, reconsider and then consider again. Tony's death was not a surprise; we'd been living with the unforgiving expectation of it for too long a time for me to be shocked and broken now, right?

At the beginning of my process, it seemed that no one had anything to say to me that made any sense. More than that, few of the people who were closest to me had ever lost anyone, and most didn't know what to say. Everyone was grieving over Tony, too, each in his or her own way, trying to deal with his permanent absence.

Despite the fact that I wanted to soothe my bleeding heart with words, I couldn't find any that made me feel better. Little that anyone else had to say was of much interest to me; I decided that I'd heard too much of everything for far too long. As a result, I sought and found a solid refuge in differing shades of silence for the first time in my life.

Keeping my attention focused on anything in the beginning was close to impossible. I took care of the cats, I moved mechanically through my days, and actively avoided all thoughts of the future. I spoke when spoken to, and rarely ventured out of my constantly-shrinking comfort zone.

And late at night, since falling asleep had become almost as much work as staying awake was once I was finally dully conscious again each day, I started reading a little to help me wind down at bedtime.

I kept myself away from Lynn's book as long as I could, on the off-chance that purposely sidestepping what she had to say would protect me from the stark realities of my new and mostly alien situation. I tried to read other books and magazines, but couldn't get interested enough or stay focused on what I was looking at. I went through at least five other books before I gave up, broke down, and resignedly picked up *Being a Widow*.

I began to read it, taking in as much as I could, which wasn't very much in the beginning. I didn't always like what she had to say, and some of what she was telling me made me unhappy and uncomfortable and even frightened about my unsteady perceptions about my future. But what she said helped me to take the initial (if stubbornly halting) steps into the truths of my own process.

Before I was a third of the way into her book, Lynn was food and drink at the end of my day. I was starving then, thirsty for someone who could understand how I was feeling, and here she was. I didn't have to talk, didn't have to tell her my story; I didn't even know for sure what my story was at that point. I let Lynn's words pour gently over whatever mood I was in, and I caught myself paying close attention to what she had to say as I tested her words against my own raw, aching thoughts and feelings. I chose to trust that she would show me better and safer and less awkward ways to walk the road I was on, and she didn't let me down.

By the time I'd devoured the first half of her book, I went through a brief but intense phase when Lynn was the only person I would listen to about how to keep breathing, or how to make it through the day in one piece.

She didn't pull any punches, and I liked that. She told me that people around me were going to say stupid but well-meaning things (they did — she even told me what the stupid things would be). She showed me how to give these well-meaning people space to help me with whatever it was that I needed. She made me feel as though she completely understood how I was feeling, what I was afraid of, how intensely angry I was (at Tony? at God? at myself?). And she gave me plenty of latitude to see that whatever I was feeling in the moment, whether it was rage or despair or fear or loneliness or regret or stubbornness or complete avoidance of just about everything, was perfectly all right.

Lynn had carefully and consciously left signposts on the road so that I could recognize them easily when I got to them at my own pace and rhythm: the various stages of grief, what to do about excessive stress and anxiety, paying attention to my dreams, how to step back into life with a little grace. She even hinted politely about the possibilities of dating and sexuality somewhere in a future I couldn't yet fathom. (I skipped that part the first time through, but went back to it a year later with a much healthier perspective.) Lynn made me feel as though she was personally determined to give me as much information and support as I needed to move through those first few months and then years without Tony.

I got to the point where I'd read something I didn't think I was going to like, and so I'd argue with her a little. "No, that can't be right, Lynn... I don't need a new social life. I'm doing just fine with the old one." (Wrong. My social life had to go through several bumpy evolutions before it felt entirely comfortable again. Too often when I got together with friends, we all seemed to be sitting around waiting for Tony to show up. It took me some time to accept the fact that my social life and the way I viewed it had to be altered and sometimes sharply modified to fit my new life without Tony in order for it to be okay for me and for everyone else, too.)

"No, Lynn," I'd grumble at her in the small hours of the night (I couldn't sleep). "I do not need grief counseling. I am not a wreck." Wrong again. I had entirely stopped sleeping. I *was* a wreck, in some basic and not immediately visible ways. In private I was having panic attacks that generated enough kinetic energy to light up Las Vegas. Argument conceded, I looked for and found a good counselor, who showed me some tools for coping. Over a period of months, the panic attacks became less frequent and eventually disappeared altogether.

It sounds a little silly, I know, but I'll tell you the truth anyway. After a while, I began to feel that Lynn Caine was a special friend of mine, a well-traveled friend who was showing me the ropes for the new trip I was on, one who was also aware that I needed to come up to speed on my own terms.

I began to look forward to the time I'd spend reading Lynn's book every night. It wasn't that I felt that I was close to her; but as a wounded, grieving soul in need of a gracious, compassionate mentor, I felt that she was close to *me*, and I blessed her for it.

The Epilogue of *Being a Widow* begins with the words "In 1983 I developed cancer."

I nearly dropped the book in alarm. Not Lynn! Not cancer! I was worried for my new friend and, with shaking hands and a sinking feeling in my chest, I kept on reading. It was breast cancer, malignant, and Lynn was setting her affairs in order, living the lessons she'd learned along the way, preparing her children and her friends for her death. She was sweet, caring and charming in the ways she freely expressed the things she was worried about, the people she loved, and what it was that she wanted from her life before it was all the way over.

Her attitude was upbeat and genuinely cheerful, and she soothed my fears for her. I felt better, because she felt better.

There's a paragraph in italics immediately at the end of the Epilogue. The first sentence reads:

> "Lynn Caine died of cancer December 16, 1987, at Columbia Presbyterian Medical Center in New York City."

I put the book down and wept, long and bitterly, for the loss of the woman who had not actually been my friend, but who had been the friend of my grieving process: a woman whose open-hearted generosity was feeding a part of me that I couldn't identify then, the part of me that wanted to and desperately needed to continue somehow after Tony died.

I lost a bit of my footing; my grief doubled for a time. I mourned the loss of a woman I'd never met but who had graciously held my hand through my own dark night.

And when I was ready, I noticed something.

Lynn had died in late 1987. Tony's cancer had not been diagnosed until 1991. In reality, Lynn had been gone four years before Tony even got sick. By the time I encountered *Being a Widow*, as a widow myself, it was 2001; she had been gone for fourteen years. Fourteen years after her death, she helped me in ways that no one else could, ways I couldn't have helped myself once the foundations of my life had finally crashed, burned, and generally evaporated.

In print, Lynn will be alive and helping people forever, the way she helped me, and the way she can help you.

I don't grieve for Lynn any longer. I smile, and am grateful for the gift of the journey she shared, and for the lessons she learned and was willing to teach.

But that's not what I meant to tell you.

What I meant to tell you is that when you choose to be ready for it, you don't have to walk the journey through grief all on your own. I had expected to, and I am glad that Lynn proved me wrong so effortlessly.

There are books of all kinds, books filled with other people's stories of loss and pain. You might believe, as I did in the beginning, that you've had enough of sad stories because you've got your own. I discovered that, strangely enough, reading or hearing someone else's stories of illness, loss and grief hooks into the stories that I carry now, and in some way the sharing of these intense experiences connects and strengthens the both teller and the listener. I tend toward bookishness as a matter of course, so reading (rather than talking) about what other people have gone through helped me, and may help you, too. The key is to find what works best for you in your process, and to go with that.

There are counselors that specialize in dealing with grief. Find someone who can help you find usable tools for getting past some of the worst of the rough spots. I did, and she was exactly what I needed at that point in my journey. Early on, she gave me a few effective tools, among them the practice of getting Tony to "go away" when my thinking so much about him and his last difficult days began to suffocate me and I literally had trouble breathing. She taught me how to make space in my head for consciously and conscientiously breathing and sleeping and being. And later she showed me how to "invite" Tony back into my perceptions slowly, gently, and without wrecking the precarious balance I was rebuilding as I made my way through each new day.

There are support groups, clubs, and entire organizations committed to helping people who are grieving. Your priest or rabbi or pastor can put you in touch with faith-specific groups. There are people around waiting to help.

You can absolutely survive the pain of loss, the grief that shatters your sleep, the loneliness of reinventing yourself for the new life you never wanted to face without your partner. Lynn said so; I believed her, and I struggled to make it all make sense for myself in a world where Tony simply *isn't* any longer.

And now I say so, too: you can survive. There's a lot of caring, loving energy out there, in many forms, to help you do it.

This weekend I'm going to go back and reread *Being a Widow* (again). It will be good to "check in" with Lynn, and see how I'm doing in this phase of my own process.

Nightingales

I NEVER MADE MUCH ROOM in my world for nightingales. It's not that I don't like the little birds. It's simply that, by process of elimination, there is so much other music I'd rather have in my life, I'll take sweet, enchanting birdsong if the opportunity naturally presents itself, but I do not go looking for it.

Nightingales making beautiful noise in the darkness reminds me of the nightingales of another variety, the Nursing variety. My mother was a Nightingale of the first order, the best kind. I knew the music that poured from her professional life well enough, had my own sense of appreciation for it, but with an unexplored sense of relief, I let it sort of slip my mind when I flew away from her nest.

I am no Nightingale. I don't have it in me, never wanted to have it in me (or anywhere near me), so much so that I seem to have fallen on the other side of the line. If I get hurt and, say, my arm is hanging by a long but seemingly sturdy thread, I'll call a doctor if it doesn't feel better by sometime tomorrow. I'm a firm believer in the power of deftly staying away from anything medical, medicinal, and messy.

Yep, and I'm the quintessential Bad Seed about the health-related issues of everyone else in the world, too. Did you have the stomach flu last week? Don't tell me about it; I don't want to know. Your sister just had a baby? There are pictures that go along with the then-harrowing and now-funny story? Keep them, both the pictures and the story. I don't want to see the video either.

The sorry truth of the matter is that I don't *like* sick people. I can't help it, really; I don't even like *me* when I'm sick. I've made a firm policy of avoiding sick people like…like the plague (ha). And I'm generally not wild about doctors, and am even less enthusiastic about nurses, as the respective breeds go. So it somehow stands to reason, doesn't it, in the scheme of things, that I'd be the one with the partner with terminal cancer?

When the initial encounter with Tony's cancer shattered our easy-going life, doctors and, of course, nurses necessarily came with the package that housed the new regime under which we lived. I was less than thrilled. But I knew how to talk to nurses, how to easily get what we needed from them, whether they were as good at their jobs as my mother was or not. I understood how the game was played, and I played it extremely well when the need arose. I had Tony deal directly with the nurses as often as possible; he didn't have a problem with them. He was as interested in their work and experiences as I was not.

We moved uncomfortably into Year Ten of Tony's illness, and eventually we got to the place where too many things were changing too quickly, and all for the worse. Our oncologist and the family doctors told us that it was time to consider hospice care. I resisted it as long as it made sense to do so: I did not welcome the idea of having nurses, professional and capable as I knew they would have to be, lurking around us.

My resistance didn't last very long. Tony started having bad episodes that worried me. The challenges, and my stress levels, were mounting. I didn't have enough information to be able to take care of him well enough on my own; I was afraid much of the time, and had questions needing answers that were staggeringly beyond my scope. It frightened me that I could no longer deal with many of my husband's needs without professional help.

The professional help of nurses.

I discussed it with him honestly. I told him that I was out of my element, that I didn't always know what was best for him. He admitted that he didn't know what to do, either. We agreed that it might be time to ask for help so we'd have access to whatever he needed.

He made it clear to me that he would do whatever I felt we ought to do, since I was being overwhelmed by the care-giving and he was finding it increasingly difficult to ignore his illness. He was specific about one thing only: if we opted to deal with Hospice, he wanted to exact a solid promise from me that he would not, no matter what happened, ultimately be sent to the hospital to die. If we were going to bring Hospice into our world (and he admitted quietly that we probably should) he wanted to die at home. He was determined to hang out with me until the very end.

I agreed immediately, without giving that final piece of the process a single thought. To this day, I still dislike hospitals more than he ever did.

So I grudgingly called the local hospice organization, which is connected to one of our city's hospitals. There was an edge to my voice as I made the appointment for someone from Hospice to come to the house, meet us, and assess Tony's needs.

The intake nurse who introduced us to hospice care was kind and smart and knew what she was doing. She was *not* tight and impersonal and distantly professional, as I'd expected. She kept the intake process moving, and was positive and helpful. If I glared or scowled at her, she politely pretended not to notice; I know now that she took one look at the open rebellion in my eyes and knew two things. First, that I was the fractious child of a Nightingale (commonly known in other circles as a "nurse's brat"). Second, she knew that I was barely coping with the present situation, frightened nearly out of my mind.

She was also fully aware that the day we signed the papers for hospice care was the day I mentally and emotionally gave up our active stance of "we're going to beat this thing," which had kept me steady and emotionally agile for years. I never said as much to Tony, but in my heart I felt that signing those papers was my concession to the painful realities of his terminal illness. It was the first time I ever admitted to myself that I was really going to lose him. The final march toward the end of our story had begun. I had, myself, initiated it with a phone call.

The best thing about our relationship with Hospice was that now I had help. If Tony had a problem in the middle of the night, and I didn't know what to do, I had access to someone on call to answer my uneasy questions. I got experienced advice, direction, and active support. I got to know nearly every nurse on night and weekend duty.

The only utterly disconcerting thing about my initial encounter with Hospice was based upon my own ignorance. When we signed up, I presumed that the nurses were going to come to the house on schedule and take care of Tony, and do whatever was necessary. I had resigned myself to this with only a minimum of grumbling. But I was wrong; what the nurses did was support me while *I* took care of Tony. My confidence in my ability to deal with Tony's needs, with his cancer in general and with nurses overall, hit the wall, hard.

Ouch.

"Maybe you could just go and hang out with *them*," I suggested to him miserably. "I could visit you on the odd weekend or something."

"You don't get to palm me off that easily, Sweetie," Tony grinned at me.

I scowled at him, and wondered about who I might be able to palm him off on, if not the nurses. I should have been able to think of *someone*; he was smart, undeniably adorable, funny, articulate, and was housebroken, too. And I'd even throw in his books and his tools as an added incentive. I asked him for suggestions for where to jettison him, and I think I was only half-kidding.

"Dream on, you brat," he chuckled, thoroughly entertained at my perplexity. He loved the notion that I'd have, as he said, "the opportunity" to deal with nurses on a regular basis. He was always in favor of me stretching beyond what I believed were my own very clear limits, and he was vastly amused at the thought that our home would no longer be a Nurse-Free Zone.

"It'll be good for you," he teased.

"Shut up," I groaned.

The Nightingales were coming, dammit. And they were tuning up their voices.

Roberta was Tony's primary nurse. She is one of the most genuinely caring people I have ever met, and she showed me very early on in our relationship that she was committed to helping and supporting Tony during the strange and difficult journey through the last stages of cancer. What I hadn't expected was that she was equally (and sometimes more) committed to supporting me through each of the layers of Tony's process. Her quieter goal was to help me to prepare for and begin to acknowledge the life I would have to live without him.

She is a small, slight woman with the heart of a lioness and an intuitive wisdom I eventually learned to trust implicitly. She has an unaffectedly sweet, grass-roots, gentle hippie-type of soul, the kind of woman who would have stayed away from the music of Woodstock only because she was on her way to register voters or be present at yet another anti-war demonstration. She and Tony, himself an active war-protester in his youth, bonded quickly; it took much longer for me to stop seeing her as The Nurse in Charge. But once I finally got over my growling, and allowed myself to get to know her, my life was richer and my world was safer because she was truly willing and entirely able to walk the dark road with us. She was in it for the duration, just as we were.

Roberta came to know us well, and was even accepted if not altogether trusted by all four of our cats.

She came to see Tony twice a week in the beginning. While I believe she sometimes let herself be charmed and occasionally fooled by Tony's debonair behavior, his disarming personality, and the fact that he was just so damned interesting and fun to talk with, she was without question the solid bridge between us and the daily repercussions of Tony's cancer issues. I watched him work hard to distract and engage her. While she was entertained by his performance (and who could blame her, everyone was entertained by Tony), she was always keenly focused on what his body was doing, where his headspace was, and what he needed on any given day.

She did her job, and true to form, Tony did his, stubbornly playing the role of *The Perfect Cancer Patient with No Real Problems*. He needed to stay emotionally detached from his illness; his denial was the strongest weapon in his arsenal. He preferred to spend their time together talking more about her than about himself. While she took his blood pressure and did her routine checks, they talked politics, the economy and ecology. He got her to tell him about how much she loved to hike, and where.

On the days when I was not at the house when she visited him, she called me at work and discussed the visit; she kept me constantly aware of what was going on with him. She observed him a great deal more closely than he realized; I was reassured by that.

As I began to know and trust Roberta over the nine months that she was an active part of our lives, she taught me how to learn to respect Tony's difficult and sometimes maddening processes for dealing with his situation. She showed me how to give him room to go off on alternative tangents that at any other time would have driven me up and down the walls a few times. She helped me to understand many of the things he was most likely thinking about but not actually saying in terms of his private concerns and fears about facing his own death. With her gentle guidance, I learned to quietly give him whatever he needed to get his internal work done.

Most astonishingly of all, despite an uncharacteristic lack of conversation on the matter from me, she understood my foundational negative issues about illness in specific, and nurses and nursing in general. She taught me by example that while my take on Nightingales was perhaps a bit too subjective, it didn't apply to every nurse on the planet. She showed me that if I looked closely enough, I would be able to look past my feelings about the noisy birds and be able to hear the sweetness of the music, which was the gift that our Nightingales brought to Tony and me with caring consistency.

One day toward the end of Tony's life, Roberta and I sat in the dining room drinking a cup of tea together; Tony was asleep in the next room. She said one of the most alarming things anyone has ever said to me:

"I was thinking about you the other day, and I decided that, based on your personality, you'd make a fabulous ER doctor."

I was horrified. I don't like blood, I don't do sick people, and I can live without the emotional bombardment of ERs. I'd been in enough of them in ten years to last several lifetimes. "You're out of your mind," I told her testily.

"No, you'd be the best!" Roberta insisted. "Here's why: you think fast on your feet, you're smart, you're decisive, you trust your instincts (and you're generally right). When you're confronted with something scary and difficult, you get mad at it but still you dive in and deal with it quickly. Then once the job is done and done well, you're more than happy to pass the post-crisis mess and stray details along to someone — make that *anyone*— else." She smiled at me serenely. She may even have winked.

I glared at her suspiciously.

"Yes," she repeated, placidly sipping her tea, "you'd be one hell of an ER doctor. Or even a nurse."

I stuck my tongue out at her, but somewhere in the back of my mind I thought she might be on to something...except that I still don't like sick people, medical people, blood and guts, and emotional upheaval. You're all very safe from me; you'll never find me in your local ER doing anything constructive. I promise.

Okay, so sometimes I'm a little slow on the uptake; it took me a while to figure out what she was actually telling me. She knew that I would not accept the words if she'd handed them to me directly. In her opinion, I was doing a very good job taking care of Tony, and she was proud of me (and probably a little startled that I kept on doing it since I made no secret of how much I didn't want to be doing it at all). She knew I wouldn't have taken her direct praise, would have denied it immediately. She understood that I genuinely believed I wasn't doing very well with the daily and nightly nursing of the beloved man who was losing his fight.

I can still hear her words, and I remember the steady, approving look in her eyes when she said them. I use them now to absolve myself when I walk too far down the road of pointless recrimination of my performance in those days. I don't beat myself up about it as often as I might have without Roberta's kind appraisal of my tortured efforts.

It was Roberta who helped me to stay together during the frightening illness-specific twists and turns of Tony's last months of life. We expected him to die several times before he actually did; he rallied rather spectacularly a time or two before he finally let go of the battle. It was Roberta who kept an eye on my stress levels, who listened when Tony made me insane on those occasions when he had both the energy and the inclination to attempt to do something that was beyond his physical capacity. It was Roberta who understood my fears and who acted as sounding board when I didn't know what to do next. In her way, she shielded me from too much information, explained what was happening as Tony moved through each new and frightening door. She answered every uneasy question, listened to every bitter concern, and taught me that honoring Tony's process, no matter how ridiculous, lame or just plain stupid I thought it was on any given day, was the very best thing I could do for him and for myself as well.

There was another wonderful woman who did much to alter my take on the magic and blessing of nurses. I didn't think she was so wonderful the first dozen times I talked with her, but I was unbelievably wrong about her. Her name is Pat, and she and I only interacted over the telephone late at night or on weekends. If something was going on with Tony that I didn't understand, or he needed something but I didn't know what it was, or I needed direction or an answer to a question, and I had to call Hospice after Roberta's regular work hours, I'd call the switchboard, and they'd connect me with whichever Nightingale was on duty at the time. At the most stressful of those times, that person was invariably Pat.

I hated talking to her.

She seemed indecisive, under-informed, way too low-key and mellow, and her usual response to my stressful situation ("Hi, he's agitated and I can't get him to settle down and he's already had all of his tranquilizer meds," "Hi, it's me again, he's sick as a dog and I can't get it to stop, and he's having too much trouble breathing") was always the same: "Okay, I think I see, what do *you* think you should do?"

I wanted to have her shot. A brief interaction with Pat made me feel like I knew far more about taking care of a terminally-ill patient than she did, and that made me crazy. I only wanted the answer, please; I'd do the work (there was no one else around who was going to do it), just give me the information I need, call out the cavalry or not, I don't care, but don't make me guess, okay???

I don't think I ever complained too loudly to Roberta about Pat, but I know I mentioned once or twice that I didn't understand how it usually worked out that I ended up with Pat on the phone when I had to call Hospice after hours.

"You're just lucky, I guess," Roberta told me with a smile. "I've never found her to be indecisive. She's an amazing person, and I respect her a lot. It's kind of funny that you don't like dealing with her; she has a lot of qualities that remind me of you."

I was not amused, and sniffed at Roberta disdainfully. "I don't need her to be my friend, I need answers when I need answers," I retorted. "I need someone effective, someone who knows what she's doing! I need someone who knows more than I do!"

I couldn't have known just how much I would need Pat later, and what a positive impact she would have on me. All I knew then was that she was not my favorite Nightingale, and I was both relieved and pleased when I called Hospice late at night and anyone else answered the phone.

It was hard for Roberta to believe that Tony was anything but an angel, that "Perfect Patient," even though she'd been a hospice nurse for well over a decade and had pretty much seen it all.

The last month or so of his life, he became agitated easily, and lashed out at me in his anger, his fear and his utter frustration. He also managed to blow up only in private, which was as annoying as hell; no one I complained to about it could believe that my mellow, easygoing Tony would ever yell at me. His fury was often difficult to deal with; he had never treated me this way. Despite my own ready temper (which I admit didn't help matters at all), Roberta helped me to understand that this behavior, too, was part of his process.

So I did not fight back too often when he exploded at me, blamed me for an imagined —or genuine— transgression. When I talked with Roberta about it, she was surprised and found it hard to believe that sweet, funny Tony was really giving me anything close to a bad time.

"You're just tired," she told me sympathetically when I spitefully tattled on him after a particularly unpleasant episode.

"He's feeling pushed too far toward the line, and I get that," I told her as reasonably as I could, "But I want to smack him."

"You're entitled to overreact," she said, and I glowered a little. She couldn't imagine that he'd actually yell at me. He was too much of a sweetheart.

So the day that she was sitting on the couch talking with him, and I entered the room and he spontaneously erupted at me, she was stunned first into silence, and then into reprimand. "Tony, I can't believe you'd shout at her like that," Roberta said, and Tony was instantly contrite. "It's so unlike you."

Yeah, it was so unlike the Tony I'd always lived with, but not so unlike anyone dealing with the levels of anxiety and physical discomfort that he was. He was only sorry that his secret was out.

There, I've said it; he would have loved to have finished out his life without having had anyone other than me see him in some of his darker, nastier moments. My Tony wasn't perfect.

Thank God.

One of the last times Tony saw Roberta, after she left the house, he looked at me tiredly and said, "Did I do all right?" which meant, did he keep up a good front so that she'd think well of him.

"Of course you did, Hon," I assured him, wishing that she could see him in that moment, too. He did not want to be a burden to her any more than he wanted to be a burden to me. He wanted her to have a good time when she came to see him, and as a result he put a good deal of his waning energy into his best showmanship. To this day I still don't think Roberta knows quite how hard he worked to make her proud of him.

Roberta told us she was taking her vacation. She planned to visit her mother, for a week, halfway across the country. I didn't want her to go; I felt strangely clingy despite my best efforts to conceal it. It had been a hard summer: Tony was declining alarmingly and then miraculously rallying, only to lose more ground afterward from the effort. We had made several intense and stressful Midnight Runs to the ER. He had a couple of terrifying adventures that I only barely survived, and we played out some stray emotionally-charged episodes that might have capsized a less-seasoned marriage. To make matters even more interesting, he took a few headers, falls that didn't hurt him too much but which shook me to the core.

I didn't want Roberta to go, but she felt confident that Tony was doing well enough at the moment that she could leave us for a week; a substitute Nightingale would be able to take care of things until she got back. I bit my lip, told her to have a good and safe journey, and only reluctantly let her go. I don't remember if I actually added "Hurry back…" but I know I said it to myself.

She knew I was worried about her leaving. She called me from the airport to touch base again that evening. "Don't forget to breathe!" she reminded me. "I'll see you in a week. Don't worry!"

That was a Thursday night.

After the worst weekend we'd had in ten years, Tony died early the following Tuesday morning.

I understood, and I didn't understand at all: Tony was dead. The battle was over. We had lost.

Caught in the smothering crossfire of my own confusion, I called the Hospice switchboard to let them know we were finished. The switchboard operator passed me to the nurse on call that night.

It was Pat.

This time I was too tired and too numb to care. I told her simply that he was gone, and asked her what I should do next. She said she would call the people from the mortuary, and she would get everything necessary in motion. Pat told me she would head for my house right away. I said that was fine (or something equally bland) and hung up the phone.

I couldn't tell you what Pat looks like. I only met her once, in the small hours of that morning as Tony lay in the bed peaceful and released at last. I have a vague sense of dark hair with strands of gray in it, and bright eyes.

No, I couldn't tell you what she looks like, but I can tell you what she felt like when she walked in the front door that morning before the sun came up on one of the saddest days of my life: she carried sweetness and calm and joy and a sense of blessed completeness with her. She quietly brought balance, warm safety, purpose, comfort, and healing energy into my dazed darkness, and she took kind, competent control of the new situation.

Pat, I learned right away, was a practicing Buddhist, another of the Flower Children who did it right, lived the life honestly and was richly spiritual in her way. (This realization has made me rethink my irritation at her constant reply of "What do *you* think you should do?" dozens of times since then.)

She very gently steered me toward my bedroom (Tony was dead in the hospital bed in the living room), and had my friend Shari, who had spent the long night with Tony and me, stay with me there.

Time froze. I kept my eyes fixed on Shari. If we spoke, I don't remember what we said. I didn't fall apart; I was paralyzed by utter exhaustion. I only remember the dull sound of my own heart, thudding heavily in my chest, and my dispassionate amazement at how much time there was in the long stretches between its tired beats.

While I sat on the bed and kept on breathing somehow, Pat was hanging out with Tony's body.

With a deep and shining respect that I had never encountered in a Nightingale before, Pat undressed Tony's body, and gently bathed it. She brushed his hair, blessed him, and came back into the bedroom to help me find something for him to wear to the mortuary.

I gave her one of his favorite tee shirts, and she took it from me with a soft smile, then returned to the living room and put it on his body, talking to him quietly all the while. When she was finished, she joined Shari and me in the bedroom.

I had not moved from my seated position on the bed; Shari was seated close by. Pat sat down with us.

She talked about the mysteries of energy and how energy does not die. I had already owned this truth but it was so lovely to hear her perspective on it in that broken moment. She deftly and gently made sure that I was going to remember to breathe.

By the time I finally walked back into the living room to where Tony's body lay, thanks to Pat I was in a better space to cope. I sat beside him on his bed and talked to him as the strange new day was born around me.

For the record, I never told Tony goodbye. We had had a lot of time to think about it, and we decided that we were both unwilling to do that. As I sat with his body, I held his hand (it was too cold), and I told him softly that I'd see him later, and I meant it. That last goodbye was never spoken; I was glad he had never said it to me. We'd ended our friendship, our love affair and our marriage exactly the way we'd agreed to: no goodbyes, not ever, no matter what happened.

It was barely enough to let me keep my defiant edge.

But that's not what I meant to tell you.

What I meant to tell you is that while I reserve the right to still keep a healthy distance from hospitals, I've mellowed considerably. I have revised my life-long stance against Nightingales, based on the unimaginable sweetness of the music that I learned to hear from both Roberta and Pat. Two entirely different women, each dedicated to the same cause: assisting and honoring the body's and the soul's journey from this place to the next, and teaching the heart left behind to find room to breathe and begin to move forward.

Roberta and her husband moved out of the area not too long after Tony died. I correspond with her periodically. One of her first letters to me reiterated how proud she was of me for the sometimes impossible job of taking good and loving care of Tony. Every once in a while, I re-read that letter; it helps me to better understand and even forgive myself for the deep feelings of doubt and insecurity I still carry about my life that final year. Roberta's sweet and protective birdsong made that time more bearable for me, and I find that I trust her now as I did then.

I never saw Pat again. A few months after Tony died, I heard that she had gone on an extended sabbatical, and was traveling in India. Somehow, I wasn't at all surprised. I remain grateful for Pat's beautiful presence on my first morning without Tony.

Yes, I've shifted my perspective on Nightingales. They're not my favorite species, and I certainly don't watch for them (and would be happier if I didn't have occasion to encounter them at all). But I've learned first-hand to appreciate and respect the healing melodies they brought into my dark nights when the saving brightness of dawn seemed much too far away.

And as my memories of Tony ebb and flow, with hurt and laughter and loneliness and hope, the remembered song of our own personal Nightingales lingers, wraps itself protectively around the depths of my sadness, and helps me to smile.

80/10/10

MY TAKE ON MOST THINGS is generally — and happily — somewhat outside of the comfortable, predictable range of what's considered normal for most people, and I like it that way. I think that what helps us each move through our own stuff, whether it's coping with grief after a devastating loss or feeling irritation at the next-door neighbor whose dog barked all night, has a great deal to do with who we are and how we choose to look at the world around us. I walk through life on many of the same roads as everyone else does; I just have a tendency to be attracted to and intrigued by different kinds of scenery along the way.

I mention this because I have several close friends who are getting married in the near future, and that has me thinking about my feelings about marriage in general, and my marriage to Tony in particular, which then gets me thinking about the essence and character of the grief I'm still working through. And I'm a little surprised and a lot entertained by how similar both experiences suddenly seem to be.

Let me show you what I mean.

Tony was the first person I'd ever been in love with up to my eyebrows. He was, from the very beginning, the most generous, loving, caring, intuitive, nurturing, gentle and charming man I'd ever known. (And for the record, he didn't change all that much over the years.)

The early stages of our romance went through all the natural paces that everyone's romances do. You know, the violins and roses, the all-night phone calls, and the lovely distractions inspired by new love. As we grew more and more comfortable together, and as the red-hot excitement of the initial infatuation calmed down (a little) into the strong bonds of love and affection, tenderness and partnership, we decided that we wanted to get married.

Once the decision was made, Tony had a great time harassing me about the less attractive side of my disposition. He made it clear that he didn't want to marry me until he saw the full force of my then-legendary temper. I was too busy being happily in love with him in the early days to get angry enough to blow the house down, so it took us a while. Once he finally saw it, though, he said he didn't want to marry anyone *but* me; he figured that his life would be just fine if the scariest thing in the world he had to deal with (and, inexplicably, he meant me) was already living in his house with him.

We moved into marriage easily, happily, and with bright hopes for the future. Life was good, and there was easy laughter, magic in all the right places, and plenty of love and room to grow in whichever directions we chose.

It didn't take me long to see the pattern of what a happy, settled, contented married life was going to mean for me. And after checking in with my friends periodically over the years about their perceptions of their own marriages, this is what I have come to believe about the genuine state of marriage in the practical world, rather than in the starry-eyed, romanticized abstract: I call it the "80/10/10 Paradigm of Marriage."

Let's be honest here: Eighty per cent of the time, you're just living your life, day in and day out, with the one you love. You're having lovely nights, of course, because, after all, you're living with the person you love best. You are moving along your individual and collective paths, and life is good most of the time. You grow and change in (hopefully) positive ways, and your relationship does, too.

You remember vaguely that no one ever told you before you and your beloved tied the knot and/or moved in together that everyday reality could be tedious sometimes, and downright boring at others. It does get a little dull, despite the countless hours of love, the hand-holding, the Friday Night Date in front of the TV with pizza. You're in love, of course, but it's probably not continuously red-hot, intense, and excruciatingly exciting, at least not the way it was in the beginning. And you come to see that that's not such a bad thing, since life tends to get busy while energy shifts and time moves forward as we change. You gaze contentedly at your spouse across the breakfast table and catch yourself admitting that s/he is definitely one of your better habits.

Over the years, the energy beneath and around the relationship glides along naturally, ebbing and flowing with the varying colors and tides of your love and your life. There aren't constant highs and lows; there's a smooth symmetry to your corner of the world that makes your loving relationship a wonderful place to be. And that's a nice thing; comfortable never felt so good as it does in a steady, happy delicious partnership that grows as you do.

It's no wonder that we spend most of our time here.

Outside of that eighty per cent of Real Life resides a full ten per cent of the time where you can't get through a minute without being fully aware of your love for your partner. It's not only about sex. It's the deeply-connected, emotional and physical sense that you carry inside that is keenly aware of just how much you love and need and want your spouse. You want her close by. It is unthinkable that you could get through the day without him. You're so happy that you're goofy with the bliss of it all. You'll do anything s/he asks of you, no matter what, just because it will make her/him smile. You haven't lost your mind, and you're entirely yourself, but you're so much more yourself because you are cheerfully and entirely in love with the best person in the world (who, miraculously, loves you back and actually lives with you!) and all is right even when things are not perfect. Together you can master any challenge, conquer any problem, handle any situation, so long as you're holding the hand of the person who completes you. This is love at its most powerful and magical. It's what you were born for. You nearly tremble with the joy of it all.

Nice, isn't it? Hold that thought for a minute.

And then there's the other ten per cent of the Paradigm. This is the time when you're not sure why you are still married to him or to her. Has she always been this much of a disagreeable shrew? Why don't you quietly arrange to send him back to his mother, and pretend the marriage never happened in the first place (even though it was ten years ago)? Ah yes, these are the nastier moments of True Love and Real Life that make you wonder why you ever bothered: the maddening (and funny to me, now) ten per cent of the marriage where you'd gladly run your loving partner over with your car three or four times to make absolutely sure that s/he has enough broken bones to effectively stay out of your face for a while. You see your relationship with a stark, cold clarity: your partner is insane. She's mean, he's emotionally unavailable, she's fat, he doesn't shower often enough, she's snippy, he's more interested in football, she's lazy, he's probably cheating. This is Love's ugly down side. The love you know with this person is not gone, it's just taken a really long coffee break. You're so angry and frustrated and unhappy that you tremble with the misery of it all.

But don't worry; once you've barked a little, and looked longingly at the car idling in your driveway while you try to come up with a clever way to lure him under it, once you've said a couple of sentences too many, threatened to leave for anyplace where she *isn't,* or thrown a rather large flower pot at his head, everything will be all right, and you'll be making up and making out before the day's over.

That's the Paradigm: ten per cent is unbelievable bliss, ten per cent completely sucks, and eighty per cent is just Life and Love, the true marriage of lovers, partners, friends and soul mates moving through life together.

I'm finding that my grief is much like this as it has moved through its phases and cycles and taken me along with it.

Once the initial overwhelming shock, exhausted anger and all the rest of it began to subside after Tony died, and I finally was able to spend more time functioning than not functioning in the world, a pattern started to emerge that I've learned to acknowledge as a grounding reminder as I deal with the loss of my partner.

Ten per cent of the time, I handle the new truths of my life extremely well: the fact that I'm alone, that I'm no longer married to my sweetheart, and that I bear the scars that the whip of his cancer left on my soul. All these things I can accept and even talk about with a grace and ease that I never imagined possible. That ten per cent of my world now is peaceful, and I find that I am unafraid of my future, and even dare to dream of a new life and new happiness. I even ponder the notion of someday falling in love again. It's a safe and happy ten per cent that I welcome whenever I happen into it.

There's another full ten per cent of the paradigm where I simply cannot breathe. The loneliness is overwhelming; without warning, hot tears bleed out of the dark, empty chasm that Tony's absence has created inside me. I feel as though I have lost every shred of my hard-won coping skills, and have to begin all over again; I stagger back to that soul-smashing place that is Day One Without Tony. I find myself struggling to get through the next hour with my newly-shattered heart intact. In this place I know that I will always be alone, forever untouched except by bittersweet memory, always longing for one more smile from the man I loved with my whole life. In the darkness I mourn him, and ache for a familiar, gentle reprimand about my evil temper.

I find myself willing to do just about anything for a single moment of impossible contact, even if it's only a dream. When I'm in this space, I cannot talk about him. I seem to remember only the last few awful days of his life, before he was gone and took a good portion of my heart with him. In these moments I move away from my friends and my responsibilities, and either wait out the process or fight to push myself through it so I can regain my balance.

That balance actively lives in the remaining eighty per cent of my private world of grief: it's not extreme, it's relatively calm. The things that happen in this paradigm are normal, natural, and the way things can play out for all of us. And strange as it may sound, there's immense comfort for me in that.

Flat tire on the freeway in the pouring rain? Lay it on me; it happens to everyone once in a while. Forgot my wallet and didn't realize it until I was at the grocery check-out? Bring it on. Serious screw-up at the office? A fatal faux pas at a dinner party? Problems with the plumbing at home? Thank God! My life in the eighty per cent range can be full of irritating, unpleasant, everyday things that I can handle. Or maybe nothing is happening at all. My days are no longer filled with larger-than-life problems, impossible decisions and life-and-death battles. I am as likely to be accosted by mundane, mind-bendingly stupid or deathly boring stuff as anyone else is, now. Isn't that great?

Tony is just as absent from this mostly-level and equalized space as he is from the other two arenas, the upside and the downside of my life as it plays out without him now. But in the eighty per cent, where life is mostly calm and normal and, when I'm honest, sometimes tedious as hell, I can hold my own, face occasional episodes of bleak sadness or of bright optimism, and continue to journey through life on my own peacefully enough.

But that's not what I meant to tell you.

What I meant to tell you is that I've met quite a few people in the past year or so who have lost their partners to fatal illness, and a good many of them, regardless of the length of time they've been without their lost loved ones, live perpetually in the zone where laughter and joy and light are as dead to them as the one who had to go away.

As much as I struggled to find tools for coping and moving on, I was astonished when I realized that there are people who've suffered terrible loss who very calmly and rationally choose not to move on at all.

One terrific woman I met has been without her cherished husband longer than she had him in the first place, and, bless her, she still has his name on the checking account, eight years after the fact. She cannot say his name without genuine, pain-filled tears spilling. She aches for him, and I in my turn ache for her sorrow. She does not date, she does not acknowledge or celebrate holidays, and has admitted to me that many of his things are still positioned in the house the way he left them the very last time, all those years ago. She bravely has gone into therapy a few times, but, deeply uncomfortable with where the process was taking her (away from her husband), she quit so she could hold on to him. She lives and grieves alone and appears, from where I'm standing, to be terribly unhappy in her own space and also in the world at large, but she says that this is how she chooses to keep her fragile connection to the one man to whom she gave her heart.

Many people continue to wear their wedding rings after their spouse has died, and they may choose to wear them for the rest of their lives. We all keep favorite pictures of the ones we've lost, and we're ever mindful of the vacant chair at the dinner table, the vast empty space in the bed. We all have to cope, in any way we can, for as long as we can, until we can find the footing that is right for us.

Everyone's reactions to losing loved ones, and how to approach life after the fact, is as individual as each of us is. While I don't think there are any wrong ways to react and respond, I'm convinced there are ways that are not the best. At the end of the day, I only know what's not best for me, and I will admit to you that I'm discovering that largely by trial and error.

I don't have the stamina or the temperament to entirely retreat from the life that's stretching out in front of me; my personal threshold of boredom is too low and easily irritated (and I've always seen that as something of a character flaw). Tony would never have wanted me to withdraw from all the things that life has to offer. If he had thought for a moment that I would lose myself in the grieving and elect to never climb out of it, he would have had some stern words for me.

Tony wanted me to be able to be happy after he was finished here. We talked about it a lot in his last months. I didn't want to have those conversations then; they were too hard, too specific, and were predicated on the fact that I was losing him, that he was going to die, and that I'd be facing my life alone. But he made me listen to him, and he made me talk to him about it. He made it clear that he expected me to not just carry on, but to carry on with a vengeance worthy of me, to enjoy life and keep on learning and growing and to find joy and peace and maybe even love somewhere down the road. He was going to die, there was no getting around that; but he wanted me to live, and to live well.

Remembering that is sometimes the best motivation for me to stay in the game and keep playing, especially in those darker times when I just don't feel up to it, when missing him and wanting him back has a stronger pull on me than does the drive to move forward and live a new life. Learning to live within the 80/10/10 Paradigm of Grief isn't anywhere near as much fun as dancing within the 80/10/10 Paradigm of Marriage, of course. But understanding the dynamic as it applies to me now has helped me to cope with the sometimes unsteady rhythms of my own process. And in coping, I am truly beginning to heal.

Roger

AFTER TONY HAD BEEN GONE for almost a year, I met Roger at a friend's birthday party. At that point I was about two weeks from a vacation in Europe; I wasn't anticipating anything other than having a good time at the party, then going home and pondering the trip and trying to pack for it.

Roger himself was a pleasant surprise. He is the brother of someone I had worked with and whose company I had enjoyed. Roger's brother and I hadn't seen each other in a long time, so when we hooked up at the party, we spent time catching up, and Roger easily joined the conversation. I can admit that my focus was on getting through the party (I am considerably less of a social animal than I appear to be) and thinking about the upcoming vacation. At some point, Roger asked for my phone number, and apparently I gave it to him; I didn't give it much thought.

So it was a surprise to me when, about six weeks later, after I had returned from Europe, Roger called me. I had trouble placing him at first, because I had somehow gotten it into my head when the preliminary introductions were made at the party that his name was "Rod" rather than "Roger." Calling him "Rod" stuck with me a little longer than I meant it to (but only embarrassed me twice).

Roger's a nice man. He's my age, and at first glance reads very much as a free spirit who carries his own unique perspective on life. I recognized my need for him right away: he was someone new to talk to! And since he hadn't known Tony, I didn't have to be Tony's Grieving Widow, I could just be me, without anyone's heavy expectations and context. I had been starved for good conversation, for ideas other than my own. Living alone with the cats, I had already perfected the habit of "going quiet," which is my personal label for going for days on end where I don't see or speak with anyone at all. I secretly worried then that I'd lose my ability and desire to talk easily with people, even the people I knew well and cared about.

So here was Roger, and he liked to talk! And talk we did, over the phone, for something close to twenty hours that first week. We had the same taste in music, and seemed to share some philosophical and political views. This seemed as good a place as any to start a friendship. We talked every evening, often into the small hours of the following morning.

During the course of the long conversations, the topic of sex came up, and I admitted easily enough that it had been a while since I'd thought about sex at all. My sex life with Tony had evaporated as his illness took more and more of the elements of his life hostage. It startled me when I realized that I had not had sex in more than two and a half years.

Eventually Roger and I talked about different levels of safe sex (and he'd had a vasectomy some years before). Then we decided to meet.

There is something to be said for being an adult and for understanding the concept of healthy mutual use. There was no pretense, and I liked that. We were going to get together, go to bed, and see what happened from there. We told each other that we were going to initiate a "friendship with benefits" and kind of make it up as we went along. Neither of us was looking for love, we were both very clear on that. This was going to be about sex.

He showed up at the house on time. He brought me flowers. He kissed me at the door, and I shook his hand playfully and laughed, "Hi, I'll be your lover for the weekend."

While I put the flowers in water, he dropped his backpack on the table by the front door. When I walked back over to him, we kissed each other, and then headed without preamble for my bedroom, where we stayed for the better part of the next three days.

What can I tell you? The sex was intense and sweet, and exercised parts of me that I'd all but forgotten about. It was amazing and electrifying to be touched again. I had managed to convince myself when Tony died that I did not need physical contact and could make myself come to terms with the idea of living without it. In point of fact, it staggered me when I considered how I'd gone so long without anyone touching me at all; my soul ached when I realized that I had tacitly agreed somehow that not being held, caressed and hugged was all right with me and that I'd completely resigned myself to the void. A couple of hours with Roger made it clear to me that I'd been cut off from any form of physical contact for far too long. I threw myself into sexual play with joyous and grateful abandon.

I did not think about Tony.

At least, not very much.

Looking back on it now, I can see that I used the sexual encounters I had with Roger to recalibrate myself; I began to remember that I was and am a very sexual person. I'd forgotten about that for a long time, and now, wide awake again, I was slowly figuring out more of the scary puzzle of who I wanted to be in my new life. I admitted to myself that I no longer wanted to be the untouched, isolated woman who had lost her husband/lover/best friend and was expecting to be alone forever. Sex with Roger reminded me that I was still very much alive, that my body knew how to give and to receive pleasure, and that it didn't take much effort to remember how to ride that famous proverbial bicycle.

I have a cheery appreciation for the time I spent with Roger, the long talks we had, and the fact that he so generously shared his body with me and accepted the sharing of mine in return. Our energy together was far from perfect, but we were to each other exactly what we had agreed to be, and that was sufficient for both of us.

I did not have to hide from myself the fact that I was still very much in love with Tony. The broad and deep line that separated sex and love at this point in my life could not have been more visible to me; I was at peace with my feelings.

The relationship with Roger, such as it was, worked for a time; he began spending most weekends with me. When we were not having sex, we were cooking together, watching movies or playing Scrabble. Once we went for a hike. And we talked.

The more we talked, the more it became evident to me that Roger and I didn't have as much in common as I would have preferred to believe; there was not as much room for a genuine friendship as I had anticipated at the beginning. It frustrated me when I recognized that Roger was fun to have around for sex but not as much fun to have around to talk with. He knew what he thought about most things, but he didn't have a thirsty mind and took most things at face value. He held on to what he believed in with both hands (which I thought was good), but he did not like it when his basic ssumptions were challenged (which is a problem for me because I challenge just about everything I come into contact with, sometimes simply for the sake of a decent discussion).

As we spent more time together, it was clear that our ideas about life were different, too different, and would not blend, merge, and fold into the easy rhythms that I dance to in each of the important relationships in my life. The lack of intellectual, emotional, political, spiritual and creative rhythm between us was not at all Roger's fault, nor was it mine; our connection was only what it was, and that was fine. I had baggage that he was not interested in sharing, and he had issues that I did not understand and did not want to have to work through with him. The biggest difference between us was that he wanted to observe life, witness it and stand safely separate and apart from it; I wanted to dive head-first into life and savor as much of it as I could get my arms around. This seems to be a common reaction for people who've lost partners, but I didn't know it at the time. I acknowledge it now, with a small but telling grin that Tony would have applauded.

The sex stayed fun, and having someone around to talk to, even if I didn't always like what he had to say, was worth it to me for a few months. Still, I grew tired of him (rather than of his function), and I knew that he was growing frustrated with me. I wondered how long we could stand it.

I didn't have to wait very long; all I need to say here is that life intervened, as it so often does. Although I was prepared to do so, I didn't have to officially end the relationship. For reasons of his own, Roger simply stopped calling.

I am a strange and sometimes antisocial creature. I cringe here as I disclose a sorry truth about myself: people are more often a habit than a need with me. Once Roger had been entirely off of my radar for a week or so, I found I no longer needed him, or even missed him very much. It was actually painless, and solved my problem with a crisp neatness that perhaps I should have been faintly embarrassed about. I went back to my life much the way it was before Roger, except I smiled a bit more often, and found myself treating myself better.

I will always be grateful to Roger for sharing himself with me for that brief period, and for understanding where the boundaries were. He never made assumptions about what I needed or wanted, he never asked more from me than I wanted to give, and his presence made it easier for me to trudge through my second Christmas without Tony.

Roger also gave one hell of a delicious body massage.

But that's not what I meant to tell you.

What I meant to tell you is that I discovered for myself that it's absolutely critical to be touched.

You don't think you're ready yet to have someone get physically close to you? I understand. But keep listening: I asked around and bugged some of my friends and acquaintances who have been through the death of partners to find out if they'd ever had a thing like I'd had with Roger. Not surprisingly, quite a few of them had, at just about the same place in their early widowhood as I had. The majority of them were, years later, very glad for the experience, grateful for the touching, had used it as a channel for their own healing and self-esteem, and were able to move on. Okay, some felt terribly guilty (at the time, and then, for years afterward), disloyal to the dead partner, and were sorry they'd done it.

Not me. Being with Roger reminded me that there were things about relationships that I loved (and sex was unquestionably one of these) and things about relationships that I didn't like so much (arguing about nothing, and having immense difficulty in communicating were high on the list here). I never felt guilty about the sex, though. I had known for a long time that, even as he was fading and getting ready to die, Tony had been pimping for me, and only half in fun. No kidding; he even went so far as to bribe several of our friends to keep an eye out for potential boyfriends for me after he was gone.

I did myself a favor. I bought myself a good back-scratcher, one of those long wooden ones. I don't think I could live without it. I actually have two: one in the bedroom and one hanging from the bulletin board in the kitchen. I figure there's no good reason to go through life without something to literally scratch your back… especially since there's no one else around to do it, and I can't reach the middle of my back without help.

I did myself another favor: I found a good massage therapist. She is wonderful. Having someone touch your skin and work the tension out of your muscles (in a professional, therapeutic, non-threatening, and non-invasive way) is healthy for your body and for your soul. We need the physical contact, perhaps even more so after our loss because we are constantly, keenly aware that there isn't anyone around in our lives any longer to touch us in any of the ways we're used to being touched. My professional massages were a little jarring initially, especially since I'd convinced myself that being touched was simply not going to be part of the program any longer, and I'd just have to get used to it. I was wrong about that.

I've learned to hug myself. It's not something I was accustomed to doing, and I don't generally do it unless I'm alone, but every so often I'll put my arms around myself now, and hold on tight. It's comforting and reassuring. Not the best hugs I've ever had (Tony was an amazing hugger), but my own arms get the job done, and that's what counts in the moment, right?

And I rely on my buddies: I have a couple of male friends, both happily married to women who are friends of mine, who are always good for a hug if I need one. All I have to do is ask. And sometimes I don't even *have* to ask.

As for sex, sometimes I wish for a lover in my life, someone I can share myself with in all the ways that matter to me. Yes, having a lover would be all right with me. It would also be all right with the absent, cherished sweetheart who can't be with me now.

It's been well over three years since I was involved with Roger. I don't know if there's another sexual relationship somewhere down the road with my name scribbled all over it, but I do hope so. I am alive, and very much awake; I don't have a problem admitting that I get hungry.

There's a great book by Betty Dodson, called *Sex for One: The Joy of Self-Loving,* that turned my head around about taking care of myself by myself. It's published by Harmony Books. If you can't find a copy, you can borrow mine.

I've made a commitment to myself to do whatever I need to do to stay connected to myself on a basic, entirely tactile level. There's no real reason not to; I think I deserve all the healthy fun I'm willing to let myself have.

I'm convinced that massages, and getting hugged and touched often, have helped me to move gently through my own physical healing process so that I can stay engaged with life.

The Uninvited Guest

THE THING THAT STRIKES ME most now, so long after the fact, is the horrible realization that when you live with someone every day, you cease to look at them. You no longer see him. In not seeing him, you miss signs and clues that, in retrospect forever after, seem unbelievably and staggeringly obvious.

That's how it was with Tony and me. We knew what we looked like physically, and we were fine with it. We looked like *us*. He gave no real attention to my chronic weight gains and losses; I didn't think much about his, either, even when he was "suddenly" unable to wear his favorite shirts. They no longer fit around his belly.

He went through a strange and thankfully brief period of time when he felt uneasy and off-balance. He lost his temper a few times (a first in our relationship, which was by this time twelve years old), but mostly he pulled inward, and didn't talk much. He was getting a pronounced beer gut, which should have told me something, but didn't, then; he didn't drink beer.

Annual checkups were no big deal. "Tony, you should get more exercise, lose the belly," our family doctor told him two years in a row.

"Okay," Tony said amiably.

He was already on blood pressure and asthma medication, and took his meds daily. If there had been anything strange happening with his body that might have put a strain on his blood pressure, or caused him difficulty breathing, we missed that signal altogether.

A few other things were going on with Tony that he didn't mention at the time, things that might or might not have warned us that something was wrong. Tony was confused by some of these issues, embarrassed by others, and said nothing, practicing his normal routine of *Wait and See*.

I had no hint that we were about to encounter The Uninvited Guest.

A week after his annual physical, we were reading in bed. Tony leaned against the headboard, and I leaned against Tony, my head resting comfortably on his "beer belly."

One moment I was deeply engrossed in my book. In the next,

I was close to literally thunderstruck as an unbidden thought streaked through my mind and startled me so badly that I jolted straight up, knocking Tony's book out of his hands as I spun around and looked at him.

Body fat is supposed to be soft and squishy. Tony's fat felt like a beach ball. Why hadn't either of us thought of this before?

As I met his eyes, and put my hands on his belly, I knew that something was very, very wrong. I also knew instinctively that things were never going to be all the way all right ever again.

I went with him to see our family doctor again. Tony and I had each been seeing him for about eight years. The doctor had never had the pleasure of our joint company before. The dynamic was a new one for him; Tony, as ever, was light and mellow and easy to deal with, while I, usually flippant and glib and moderately self-deprecating, was instead intense and focused. I all but battered the man with questions and concerns.

It was obvious to all of us that there was a problem. For what turned out to be the first time, he actually probed Tony's abdomen with his hands, and did not look pleased when he was finished. In that examining room, (although of course I had seen Tony naked with delightful regularity) I realized that Tony's arms and neck and legs and back and hands were very thin; under the room's cold fluorescent lighting his belly seemed even bigger than I thought I remembered.

"I've been dressing to cover it, so it wouldn't seem so fat," Tony mentioned lightly, by way of explanation.

The doctor arranged for an immediate ultrasound, and he went with us for the test. It was clear to Tony and me, to the doctor, and to the ultrasound technicians, that there was something unwelcome in Tony's abdomen, but that ultrasound told us (and them) absolutely nothing.

Before I could make too much noise, our doctor ordered a CT Scan, which Tony had the next day. After the scan, which turned out to be the first (and the toughest) of more scans than I can count now, I could feel our doctor's tension as he touched my arm and advised me: "Get out of town for a few days, go see friends or take a short trip. I want you to stay busy. We won't have results from the scan for a few days, and I don't want you to sit at home and make yourselves crazy. Go have fun, and then when you're back, we'll have some answers."

Uh-oh.

I made a phone call to one of the women in my life who is a true sister of my heart and my soul. "Jane," I croaked, trying to not cry, "I think we're in trouble. Can we come and see you for a couple of days?"

Jane lives three hours away. The person that I was then, the badly-frightened and desperately-obedient woman (who just wanted something to make everything I was suddenly afraid of all better), packed a bag, pushed Tony into the car, got a neighbor to agree to feed the cats, and fled to south Jane's house. I drove like a maniac all the way, trying to outrun the fear that had been uninvited but which had come to stay.

The only thing I specifically remember now about that time at Jane's is that at some point Jane and I went for a long walk alone (no husbands allowed!), and told each other our troubles. We let our hair down as usual; we each had something to cry about, and we cried together, for ourselves and for each other. And then we went back into her house and coped with our stuff for the rest of the weekend.

When Tony and I returned home, and went back to see the doctor the next day, he had nasty news for us. Tony had a tumor in his abdomen, a big one. No one was saying the word "cancer" but everyone was thinking it. The tumor would have to, of course, come out. Our doctor had already talked to the man he felt was the best surgeon at the medical center, and he gave us his name and told us that an appointment had already been set up for a half-hour later. We went silently to the surgeon's office.

The surgeon was crisp and professional, suave and self-assured in that way that successful surgeons are. Normally that would have bugged the hell out of me, but that day I found myself grudgingly grateful for it. He was polite, and explained what he knew about our situation and what would happen next. He told Tony that the surgery would be risky because the tumor was so large, but that he was confident that he and his team could get it out of there.

The surgery date was scheduled, Tony and the surgeon shook hands, and we went home.

It seems odd to me now that the complete implosion of the happy world that I knew — my marriage, my way of looking at life, the way I perceived myself and what I was capable of doing, my perspective on our future, my faith in justice and sanity and the rightness of things, my sense of myself, and most importantly, how I saw my sweet, strong Tony — all of these things were shattered, crushed and irreparably broken that day. The spontaneous devastation took place in a matter of moments, and for all its destruction, it never made a sound.

We checked Tony into the hospital the night before the surgery. A few of our friends knew what was happening, but Tony wanted to keep it mostly quiet ("until we have something interesting to tell everyone," he said with a wink). I would have given him a bad time, but I was having difficulty thinking and breathing at the same time.

I hung out with him in his room on the Oncology Ward that night. I couldn't make myself say the word then; I simply referred to it as "that place." We chatted about domestic things, staying very far away from the realities that each minute on the clock drew us closer to. I stayed with him while a nurse gave him a shot that put him blissfully to sleep; when she left, and he was snoring lightly, I sat on the bed beside him, held his hand, and told him the things he hadn't wanted to hear and I hadn't wanted to say while he was awake. I told him about the things I was afraid of. I told him that I thought we could trust the surgeon to bring him through the procedure. I told him how much I hated the fact that I knew that our life had been changed and would continue to move in directions that I didn't trust because I didn't know how to see them looming in front me. I told him how much I loved him, and that I expected him to stay with me even if things went badly in the operating room. Then I told him two jokes, kissed him with a vengeance, and left his room.

On my way out, a couple of nurses talked with me briefly, and then asked me to join them in the back room of the nurses' station. Ever suspicious of Nightingales, I followed them, we sat down at a small table, and they began to ask me questions. Had our doctor and the surgeon answered all of my questions? Yes. Did I understand how long tomorrow's surgery would probably last? Yes. Did I have someone coming to stay with me in the surgery waiting area? Yes. Had the surgeon or his staff made it clear to me that Tony only had a twenty per cent chance of surviving the procedure?

WHAT???

Two nurses whose names I never knew held my hands across the table and explained things to me that had not been mentioned to me by the doctors. The nurses described, based on Tony's chart notes, what was expected to happen, and what might happen, and what the plan was. If this happened and they found this, then here's what the next logical step would be. But if *this* happened, and this happened next, then that meant this other thing. And if he died on the table, then, not much else would be happening. They were angry that I hadn't been told much about what I was facing.

I sat at the table between two very kind nurses, and cried harder than I'd ever cried in my life.

Later that night (perhaps it was already officially morning), I drove home wrapped in the numbness that I recognize now as part of the standard-issue wardrobe for people who have to live in and move through intense emotional overload. It was a good thing my car knew the way home; auto-piloting the trips to and from the hospital would eventually become standard procedure, although I didn't know it then.

I went home, sat in my living room in the dark, and tried to understand how Tony and I had arrived at the edge of the precipice we were about to fall from. It was too surreal to get my head around, but my heart ached miserably and my hands shook with apprehensive fear in a way that told me that whatever the hell this was, it was real. Too real.

The Uninvited Guest brought his luggage into our lives, and looked around for a room with a good view.

I can only tell you a few things about the day of Tony's first cancer surgery. One is that Kim and Aaron were present through the entire thirteen-hour procedure, and never left me; they knew

Tony was under the care of the surgical team, and could do nothing to help him, so they put their energy into keeping me company, keeping me occupied and not letting me drift too far into scary territory. They were wonderful. They'd been married as long as we'd been married, and we'd been close for years. Kim is a tall, big-framed man who is among the gentlest people I've ever known. I'd worked with him for several years and we'd become good friends, and eventually brought his fun and funny wife Aaron and Tony together into the mix. Over the years, Aaron and Kim had become family to us. Never more so, I see now, than during cancer surgery. They cared and worried and ached and feared and lost about as much sleep as I did.

Another thing I can tell you is that I made two phone calls that day, one to my mother, and one to the woman who, throughout my life, has always managed to balance out my conversations with my mother and make me feel better.

We got progress reports every few hours from the surgical team, and we gratefully acknowledged that Tony was still alive (I had told Kim and Aaron about the chat the nurses had had with me the night before). Apart from that, the specifics of that eternal day is a long, grayish blur to me.

Eventually we were told that Tony was in the recovery room and was holding his own. And when he was taken to the Intensive Care Unit six hours after that, we were finally allowed to go see him.

As we walked into the ICU, I made a startling discovery: I was terrified of seeing Tony. I didn't want to be in ICU, I didn't want him to be in ICU, and I was afraid that what I was about to see was simply what was left of my husband, not the man I loved and lived with, but instead some shadow of what he would be before he faded and flew away from me forever.

Kim and Aaron were immediately aware of my panic, and took positions on either side of me, each with an arm around me. We stopped at the nurses' station and asked to see Tony (we fibbed and said that Aaron was Tony's sister and Kim his brother-in-law, so they could get in). We were given a bed number, someone vaguely pointed the way, and we moved through the unit in search of my heart.

My eyes found him first, seconds before theirs did; I immediately recognized his feet at the end of his bed. I was so relieved at seeing something I knew was Tony that I hurried toward the bed, which was surrounded by those bed-sheet-curtained walls that provide a weak illusion of privacy.

Yeah, the feet were Tony's, as familiar to me as my own. This was a good thing, because the rest of him wasn't much like Tony at all.

He still had brown hair, and it was the right length, but the rest of Tony looked like someone I'd never seen before. His face was badly swollen because of the heavy amount of fluids that had been pumped into him during the long surgical and recovery processes. His hands were swollen, too. He looked unbelievably uncomfortable, and I reacted badly until Aaron said calmly, "That's how he's supposed to look. The swelling will go down soon, don't worry about it."

Aaron sat on the bed and took Tony's hand, while I stayed glued to Kim. Aaron patted Tony on the hand and face. "Tony," she said brightly, "Wake up. You've got company." She was not alarmed by how he looked, or by the number of tubes running in and out of him, or by the monitors.

"Are you *nuts*?" I hissed at her in panic. "Leave him alone! Let him sleep!" I told myself that he should stay unconscious for the duration; he'd like it better that way. The truth is that I was absolutely terrified at the prospect of dealing with him like this. I buried my face in Kim's shirt, and he held me tight.

"Tony," Aaron said again, stroking his hair, "Open your eyes and look at me." Tony and Aaron had been close for a long time, and had a special bond, as Kim and I did, and do to this day. In typical Tony fashion, at Aaron's request, Tony opened his eyes and looked directly at her. "How are ya, Honey?" she said to him gently.

He squeezed her hand, smiled at her, and closed his eyes. Not entirely satisfied, Aaron reached over for me, Kim pushed me gently toward her, and Aaron gave me Tony's other hand. "Tony, your sweetie's here. Show her that you're awake. She needs to know you're in there."

Tony opened his eyes, got them to focus on me, made a movement that was probably supposed to be a wink, smiled slightly, and went back to sleep.

We stayed another five minutes, Aaron and I each holding one of his hands, Aaron chatting and Kim talking softly to him while I watched them all with a silence I couldn't pull myself away from. I envied how easy Aaron was with the post-surgical version of Tony. She had had too much personal experience with surgical procedures in her own life, and was mostly undaunted by this. I admired her ability to ignore the tangible as well as the intangible horrors of the situation; I even envied it a little (which is ironic now). No, I didn't say much that night; I was too busy clinging to his hand as if it were my last link to the life I had known prior to the arrival of The Uninvited Guest.

The next weeks were full of blindingly unreal realities that needed to be faced. Tony predictably got pneumonia almost immediately after the surgery, and while he skirted death a little too closely for my taste, he got better. He spent a week in intensive care, then a week in a regular room in the hospital, where he got stronger, moved around, and was well enough to go home. Then he began his difficult twelve-week recovery period, and we tried to come to terms with the harsh new facts of our life.

The tumor the surgical team had removed from my husband's body had weighed in at twenty-eight pounds, and at that time was the largest tumor removed from a male patient who had lived through the procedure. (This bizarre record was broken later; Tony was both relieved to be "off the books" and also sorry for the man who ended up with the title.) The surgical team was able to remove the tumor intact; they placed it on a gurney and photographed it. At that time, not much was known about this rare form of cancer, which was duly identified as *retroperitoneal liposarcoma*. It's malignant, and does not require chemotherapy or radiation because it's a relatively slow grower. The tumors were made up of the same kind of human chemistry as body fat, which is why the disease didn't show up in Tony's blood tests or his ultrasound. The only way it can be easily seen is in CT Scans and MRIs, and for that reason, our family doctor told us, people often carry it around for several years and don't know it, having to wait for some other problem to appear before they get to a doctor and get it diagnosed. Our surgeon had never encountered it before he took it out of Tony; he had only seen it in medical textbooks and journals. It doesn't metastasize like so many other varieties, for which I was always more than grateful. The only way to be (temporarily) rid of this insidious cancer is to cut it out, and take a little marginal tissue with it.

The surgeon and the family doctor talked to us a lot in those first weeks. Tony's cancer cells would form into tumors, and then grow. And grow some more. He would be free of them after each successive surgery, but he would only be free of them for a time. Ultimately they would get aggressive and at some point would be deemed inoperable, and then Tony would die.

His life expectancy, at first blush, was put at two years maximum.

By the two-year point, with two surgeries under his belt, his survival estimate was pushed out to five years from the original diagnosis. By the five-year point, Tony had survived a third surgery and was doing well. After the five-year point, the doctors unanimously turned the damned clock off, and kept their estimates to themselves.

I'm thinking now that I should have taken bets on how long Tony would be able to beat the odds and stay in the game; I'd have made out gorgeously. He survived a total of five harrowing surgical procedures and their unpleasant aftermaths, and for the most part, he lived a full, rich ten years and one week after the first operation.

I would have preferred to have Tony with me every day for the rest of my life. All the time in the world would not have been enough for me to share with him, but we were constantly aware of what the fact of his cancer meant in our lives, and we tried to live accordingly.

By tacit agreement, we chose to live as well, as genuinely, and as happily as we could for as long as we could, despite the vigilant presence of The Uninvited Guest.

But that's not what I meant to tell you.

What I meant to tell you is that I have a tea towel that was given to me by a friend, long before Tony got sick. People who know me maintain that it could never have been created for anyone but me. They say it's too accurate to be amusing.

I neither confirm nor deny the allegation. I will only tell you that it is framed, hangs silently on a little-noticed wall in my house, and that I smile every time I see it.

On the towel is a picture of a teddy bear, seated, wearing a party hat. There is confetti falling gently in the air around him. Under the teddy bear is the following:

Party Rules:

1. Invite lots of guests
2. Lay in a big supply of honey
3. Disinvite the guests
4. Eat the honey

I can't help but think about how many times I loudly disinvited The Uninvited Guest from the party that was my life with Tony. But it wouldn't leave. Even when it was either deeply asleep or away on vacation (once, for almost three and a half years), the knowledge of its presence, and the danger it represented, never left my awareness. I couldn't deny its damned existence the way Tony did.

The Uninvited Guest didn't leave my house until Tony himself did, in the dark, small hours of a sad morning in the coldest autumn my soul had ever known.

Will this particular Guest come back, uninvited as before, and settle in to a room a little closer to the one in which I sleep? You never know; it might. But I've learned some things over the years since I first met it that may make any potential encounter a little less horrible. For *me*, anyway.

I hope it stays away, for the rest of my life; I don't need to see it again. Still, if it shows up after all, uninvited and unwelcome but present nonetheless, there's a lot of honey stashed away in my pantry for the next party.

Pain is Pain is Pain

TODAY I HEARD THAT A woman with whom I am only slightly acquainted is dealing with sudden, terrible news: her husband has been diagnosed with metastasized pancreatic and liver cancer.

There was a time, not all that long ago, when I presumed that hearing about horrible, sad things like this would have no genuine impact on me, especially stories that ended with the word "cancer." I've long since moved beyond that nasty little word's ability to genuinely hurt or frighten me.

I told myself today that I could be sympathetic to this woman's situation, but that I would be protected by a keen sense of *been there/ done that* which could (please) insulate me and keep me from any degree of personal empathy. I could care, certainly, but I could care from a self-prescribed, safe distance. Having touched, heard and felt most every erratic and grinding note in the cacophony of the cancer experience I shared with Tony, I do not easily or willingly return to that space. I should be relatively immune to it.

Shouldn't I?

Okay, I'm not so immune. I find my thoughts sneaking back to what this woman's world must feel like. And while I can't know all of it, because she owns her individual journey as I own mine, I think I have a pretty good idea about what she's thinking and how she's feeling right now.

All I can do is pray for her, send her some kind energy, and make myself available in the event that she ever wants to talk. It doesn't seem like very much on the surface, but I know better.

And I've been thinking, and remembering.

On the morning of Tony's second, or maybe it was the third, cancer surgery, I was well into Day Three of one of my legendary, murderous sinus headaches. Before I'd managed to stagger out of bed, I already felt like Hell on Horseback. I had been decidedly miserable for two full days and two very long nights. Day Three was promising to be particularly unpleasant; I was going to be spending it in the hospital's surgery waiting room under not-too-helpful fluorescent lighting, surrounded by the tension of waiting through another all-day cancer excision procedure, and making best efforts not to cross bridges I didn't want to approach in terms of what was going to happen next.

I knew I was in trouble that morning; acupuncture works well to relieve and also to fend off my particularly intense brand of sinus headache, but the guy I saw for that was out of town. There are certain interesting combinations of over-the-counter drugs that can kill my headache if I catch it quickly enough. If I don't deal with the headache as soon as it makes itself known, there's not much else that gets rid of it, or even relieves enough of it to matter. For whatever reason (and I'm laughing a little here, since that reason was Tony's pending cancer surgery and naturally all of my energy was focused on him and on getting us both ready for it) I didn't take the time to deal with the headache, so it greedily took up throbbing residence in my already overly-occupied head.

I have learned over my years to function efficiently (and perhaps a little stubbornly) regardless of whatever else may be going on in my day. So it was no surprise to Tony that despite my evil, wicked and (unfortunately for me) physically nauseating headache, I drove us to the hospital, got him checked in, hung out with him in Pre-Op and kept him company while we waited for the show to start. Then I sat in the waiting room with some of our friends for the next nine or ten hours.

I felt lousy, but by this time the headache was at the point where all I could do was live with it until it decided to go away. It made its nasty presence known whether I was napping, eating, staring into space, or making phone calls to anxious friends, reporting on Tony's progress in surgery.

By the time I saw Tony in the Recovery Room, some eleven hours after we'd checked him into the hospital, even the doctors thought that I looked more ill than Tony did. So did the friends who moved in and out of Intensive Care that night, and the friends that visited Tony in his room the next day, which was my Day Four of the Horrible Headache.

Here's the funny part: even as the headache began to dissipate (so slowly!) by the end of Day Four, I found that I was madder than hell at our doctors, at our friends, and at Tony himself.

And here's why: the doctors knew I was in considerable pain with the wretched, torturous headache, but that didn't matter. I was not the headliner that day. In the Recovery Room while Tony came out of anesthesia he needed to be watched; then we were in Intensive Care while Tony was being monitored and checked post-op, and the doctors and nurses and technicians were there to meet Tony's needs. I understood that. I embraced it, and was, as always, thankful for it. And I *hated* it, at least this time around. I was hurting, and rather spectacularly, too, but the focus was of course on relieving *Tony's* pain.

Our friends knew by looking at me that I was in far worse shape physically than I was emotionally. Isn't it strange how you get used to the surgical processes and find a bizarre comfort in the familiarity of it all, before things have a chance to get interesting? Everyone around me was talking about Tony's pain and the cancer and where it was located and how long the surgery was…you get the idea.

And I was furious with Tony himself, because while I was solitarily dealing with the grueling, unbending mercy of Day Four of a terrifically eye-splitting sinus headache, he was completely under anesthesia (no pain), then he was being watched carefully by the ICU staff (who made sure he felt no pain), and once in his room, the nurses made sure he was in (you guessed it) no pain.

And that was wonderful, except for the sorry fact that I was in mind-bending agony, and I could do nothing whatsoever about feeling better as I held the totally relaxed and utterly pain-free hand of my peacefully-sleeping husband.

It was all I could do not to bite him. Hard.

But that's not what I meant to tell you.

What I meant to tell you is that pain is pain is pain.

You think that's not profound?

Many of us were brought up in a religious tradition that tells us something I've always found more than a little alarming: "Suffering is good for your soul." We're taught this from the time we're small, and we buy into it as blindly as we buy into everything else we're taught early on. Sometimes we don't realize it, or question it for decades, and even then we seem to have traces of it stuck to the insides of our heads after we have evolved into the people we want to be. Suffering is good? I'm not thinking so. If you were to make a list of the top one thousand things in the world that you could personally identify as a good thing you'd opt for in your life, I'm willing to bet you just about anything that suffering would not make the list anywhere. You'd have to be insane. Masochistic. Something. Suffering is good for your soul??? Where did they get this stuff?

Let's be very clear here: while I acknowledge that it can sometimes be a teacher, suffering and its unpleasant sister-in-law, pain, is not good for your soul. Nor is it good for your body, your mind, or your spirit. For my money, anyone who actually believes that it is good for you probably hasn't suffered all that much, or has watched helplessly as someone he or she loves does the suffering.

What can we say about pain? It *hurts*. That's about all there is to it. Sometimes you can work with it, function around it, live through it, learn from it. I'm good with that. What I'm not good with is the notion that in its more dramatic forms, it can mercilessly, unceasingly monopolize every hour of a person's day, every moment of awareness, every dark breath, until endless pain is all that is left of a life that would rather be doing anything else. That's just wrong, and someday I'm going to have a long talk with God on the subject.

Pain is pain is pain. I don't think my pain is any more or any less significant or, um, *painful*, than your pain is. What I feel about the loss of Tony is no more or less devastating than what you feel about the loss of your beloved partner.

You own your pain, whatever it is, and I own mine. Is my killer sinus headache more painful than your toe, which you've just dropped a hammer on? While in my more self-absorbed moments I'd dearly love to think so, the answer is an indisputable NO. There's no comparison; pain is what it is, and it's entirely specific to the situation in which it comes to us, wholly unique in how it touches (or grabs or strangles or shreds) us.

Is how your body feels after a fall from a thirty-storey building more painful than how mine feels during a monstrous, blinding, four-day sinus headache? It could be. It might *not* be, though; you may have a higher threshold of pain than I do—and I'm willing to bet that you'd get better drugs. Comparing pain, whose is worse, whose is deeper, whose is heavier, whose is uglier, whose is more far-reaching, is pointless. Pain is pain is pain.

Pain hurts. That's all; it just *hurts*.

After Tony died, my life moved of its own accord through exhausting periods of complete disinterest in the things around me. This went on for weeks, but over time I managed to resurface. In my more focused moments, I wanted to hear what was going on in the lives of my friends, what was happening with them, the good, the bad, the gossip. I wanted to hear every detail; I was sick to death of the numbing silence whispering its way through my now-solitary days and nights.

But I wasn't getting a lot of input from people in those early days, and it didn't occur to me why this was so, until a girlfriend spontaneously burst into nearly hysterical tears over tea one day, right in the middle of a calm conversation. She successfully scared the hell out of me.

"My God, what's wrong?" I asked, worried.

"I had to have my cat put down last week," she sobbed.

"Murphy's gone?" I was stunned and very sad. She and Murphy had lived together for more than ten years. "Why didn't you tell me this last week?"

I wasn't prepared for her answer: "I couldn't come to you and tell you about Murphy, not after what you've just gone through with Tony..."

Thunderstruck, I did the only thing I could do, being me; I blew up at her. "Are you insane? I was the one who helped you pick Murphy from his litter! I know how close you two are...were—and you didn't come to me and let me help you?!? Are you out of your mind? You went through a terrible and frightening and sad time and didn't even let me know you guys were in trouble? What's wrong with you? I thought we were friends!"

I was beside myself with frustration, shock and anger, until I glared into her teary eyes and saw what she'd been thinking, what everyone pretty much thinks when someone else goes through a terrible, show-stopping, life-altering, frightening experience: she didn't think for a moment that her loss of her sweet cat measured up to my loss of my sweet husband. In my view, it absolutely did measure up; how could it *not*? If these things actually have true metrics (and I'm not at all convinced that they do) how could her loss be any less devastating than mine? Because she hadn't told me right away about losing Murphy, she had suffered alone; from her perspective on the scheme of things, which was based on the screwed-up way we're all taught to perceive whatever reality is, Murphy's death had to be of less significance than Tony's death, didn't it?

I stopped shouting, closed my mouth, and opened my heart.

And with grief streaming wetly down my face for the loss of her cherished Murphy, I showed her just how wrong she was.

The woman for whom terminal cancer has become a new and harsh reality is weighing heavily on my heart at the moment. I ache for her; I know what much of the road ahead looks like for her, and it's not pretty. I admit thinking about her situation has got me remembering the day I first understood what was happening with Tony, and while I hate the memory of that ugly day, revisiting it also hooks me back into the Collective Consciousness, reminds me of my own fragile humanity, and of yours. More than that, it allows me to make myself available to share some hard-won courage and emotional stamina with anyone who has need of it today.

Pain is pain is pain. It sucks; we do not have to like it, but there it is. We all have to deal with it, in its various colors and quantities and textures and disguises, all along our journey. We have very little control over when it comes, why it comes, and what it does to us while it's with us. What I feel, and how intensely I feel it, is my issue; what you feel, and how intensely, is yours. I can—and I do—respect that.

Maybe what we need to do is learn to acknowledge our own pain, and in so doing, learn to recognize *each other's* pain so that we can share the areas that overlap in our common experience. Then perhaps we can get to the place where we can understand each other more readily, and care about each other a little more genuinely.

It would certainly make the journey easier.

The Other Lynn

IF YOU LIVE A RELATIVELY connected life, one that allows you to see, acknowledge and appreciate the natural flow of energies not under your control, it's easier to see and accept the blessings that people bring into your life, even if you can't immediately see the value of their presence there.

I had always felt that I had a good handle on controlling who came in or passed out of the boundaries of my little universe; I consider myself an above-average gatekeeper. At that time, however, I had yet to learn that I actually have very little if any control over much of anything, especially about who strolled into my day bearing gifts I didn't know I needed.

Tony and I lived in what had once been a sweet little upstairs duplex at the end of a long row of duplexes stretching down a quiet, dead-end street. Over time, the neighborhood had disintegrated into a moderately dangerous area. Where there had once been families with small children in a well-kept and peaceful environment, there now were drug buys, crack houses, thefts and even shootings much too close to home. Our landlord had let the place fall into sorry disrepair, and I have to admit that our cute little duplex and the grounds on which it sat had decomposed through the years into something that looked, from the outside, to be a sad rat-trap in a bleak, tired and unsafe place. It was clear that we had to move out of there.

We had never owned a home, for reasons that aren't important any longer. Tony was away on business when I woke up one morning and was ready to look into the possibility of buying our first house. Well, my first house. We knew that Tony wouldn't be around for a lot longer so it would be his only house. The thought tore at me even as I started to feel excited and hopeful at the prospect of house-hunting.

My husband and I talked it over, long-distance, and we decided that I would be doing the house-hunting alone.

My friend Sheila's sister-in-law is a realtor. Not just a realtor, but a star realtor (the woman wins awards and recognition all the time, she's that good). I had never met Lynn, but had heard about her from Sheila off and on in the course of normal conversation.

Lynn had had a terribly hard road. Lynn's first husband, the father of her children, had died of cancer tragically young. Lynn's second husband had died of cancer, too, several months before I met her.

Knowing what Tony and I were facing, I told Sheila over lunch that maybe I shouldn't call Lynn about houses. It didn't make sense to me to have any kind of relationship with a woman who had had to live through the pain, heartache and loss that Lynn had, since that's where I was ultimately heading with Tony. Taking her anywhere near the life I was living seemed cruel and selfish, and I didn't want to do that to anybody. I said as much to Sheila.

Sheila eyed me with that kind yet subtly shrewd way she has, and said, "Don't you think Lynn should be the one to decide that?"

I sighed. This was not in my game plan (I was big into game plans in those days). I didn't want the responsibility of bringing anything painful to this woman I hadn't even met.

Maybe I was a little afraid to meet her, too, frightened by what I might see when I looked into her eyes, the haunted look of a woman from whom love had been so malevolently taken, twice. I did not want to play. I was certain of that.

With a smile that I have learned over the years to trust implicitly, Sheila gave me Lynn's telephone number.

I called Lynn that evening, and the rest, as they say, is history. It's *my* history now, and I cherish it.

Lynn was, and is, pure magic. We talked on the phone about what I wanted in the new house. I told her during that first call that I was a little worried about dragging her through some heavy emotional territory that might be painful to her. I remember that she made a small sound that might have been a wry chuckle; she told me that it was all right, she could handle it. In that moment, she was more concerned about the road I was walking; she had already been there and tasted the worst of it. At the time, I could not understand how that road had lost the power to frighten or hurt her.

And that was that. We agreed to meet the following Saturday; she would bring some listings, and we would go look at houses together. She wanted me to be very clear about the things that were "must have" about the house I wanted to buy.

That was easy for me. I'm claustrophobic; my soul needs light and space on a deep, essential level. Tony and I had been living in a dark, cramped place for a very long time and I had hated it. Light and breathing space would be an absolute must. We also had four indoor-only cats who needed room to run around. I wanted three bedrooms, two bathrooms, a big kitchen, all large living areas. I insisted on a separate garage for all of Tony's art stuff and related junk. I needed a back yard to putter in. Oh, I wanted light, lots and lots of light.

Lynn told me later that she had had grave doubts about the notion that we would find anything close to what I really wanted in my price range, but she very kindly kept her experienced reservations to herself, and let me enjoy the adventure. She came prepared with the stack of listings, and she arranged them in order by location so that we could drive around in a relatively efficient fashion and look at the houses.

The first house, the one sitting at the top of that stack of listings, was inviting from the moment we pulled into the driveway. I looked at Lynn and said something about it being "nice enough." We got out of her car, walked up the two steps from the driveway, and approached the front of the house. She unlocked the door and stepped aside, allowing me to enter first.

It was late September, and afternoon sunlight was generously pouring through the large picture window in the living room, the sliding glass door in the dining room, and the two huge skylights over the kitchen. There was more natural light in that one living area than I had seen in my rat-trap over all the years Tony and I had lived there. I had only been in this one large living room, dining room and kitchen space with its blazing light, but I knew within two breaths that I wanted this house.

"This is my house," I told Lynn in a whisper. I turned to look at her, and she seemed to be as amazed as I was.

"Wow," Lynn said, looking around. No one says "wow" like Lynn does. I heard surprise, relief, approval, smiles, amazement, recognition and challenge in her one syllable. I couldn't have agreed with her more.

We walked though the house together. It was a rambler, built in the late 1950s. The kitchen counter was, God help us, electric yellow (which I admit may have accounted for some of the initial brightness that drew me in). There was a small bathroom by the bedrooms and an even smaller half-bath at the other end of the house. But there was a separate garage, a good-sized master bedroom, a small room that could serve as Tony's office, and a much larger room that Tony eventually convinced me to take as my office. A third small bedroom could be a guest room. The back yard was big enough to please me, and the house stood near the end of a cheerfully quiet, dead-end street.

I toured the back yard and visited the huge cedar trees that lined one side of it. I liked them at once.

Coming back into the house to see Lynn, I told her confidently, "This is the house. This is what I want."

She looked at me thoughtfully. "You've only seen *one house*. You need to look at some more before you can make a decision."

No, I didn't. "No, I don't," I told her. "This is the one. It's almost exactly right. It's perfect. Let's make an offer."

Lynn insisted on taking me to a few other houses, even though I didn't want to; she pointed out that she wouldn't be doing her job if she let me buy the first house I'd clapped my eyes on, and for that reason alone I let her drag me away from the rambler. She walked me through two or maybe three more houses before I looked at her and said, "Let's go back to *my* house."

She took me back, I walked through it again, and found myself dreaming of living there. I wanted this house, and was determined to have it. We wrote up the paperwork, and the offer was made.

Later that evening, although it was kind of against the rules, I drove back to the house alone. I walked into the back yard, sat on the back step and looked around possessively. I imagined the garden I would create, and saw myself hosting barbeques on the patio with Tony.

As I sat there, a dog in the yard next door moved to the fence and barked at me. I went over and introduced myself. "Hi," I grinned.

She stopped barking and studied me warily in the darkness. "I'm your new neighbor."

The long and the short of it is that Tony and I bought that house. It's not perfect, but it's perfect for me. I don't mind confessing that Tony never truly liked the place, but he didn't complain about it too much, for the obvious reason that he was not going to be living there for very long (although we never actually spoke those words to each other). The bottom line is that he decided, in typical Tony fashion, to be happy that I was happy with the house. In the end, that was enough for him.

But that's not what I meant to tell you.

What I meant to tell you is that despite my original (and somewhat adamant) feelings about staying away from Lynn because I didn't want the nasty cancer realities of my life to roll into hers and cause her pain, Lynn turned out to be one of the greatest blessings of my life during Tony's journey out of it.

I'd like to state for the record that my motivation was to protect her, honestly. It had only a little to do with my sometimes overactive need to control my environment and thereby protect myself. But Lynn made the choice to come into my life, despite my reservations; I'm so happy that she did.

I'm guessing that it was readily apparent to anyone who knew me at all how very frightened I was at the prospect of losing Tony. But it was more than that. I was terrified of the *process* of losing Tony: not just the emotional stuff, not just the staggering activity of taking care of him (which I felt thoroughly unqualified and largely unprepared to do) but the actual right-there-in-your-face death itself. I couldn't imagine what it would be like, and much of my fear centered on my potential inability to handle the event itself. I kept my fears from Tony; he had enough to carry without trying to comfort me about something he didn't have a handle on, either. He'd never seen anyone die; the first death in his experience would be his own.

Over the months that followed our purchase of the house, Lynn and I kept loosely in touch. During that time, she got to know Tony a little, too.

And one day, when we were alone having tea, she said softly, "When you get to the point where you want to know something about what it's going to be like, we'll talk."

I didn't want to hear it; I just didn't want to know. And I didn't want to take her back through her own memories of the deaths of the two men she'd dearly loved and shared her life with. I wrapped myself tightly in the slightly warped illusion that if she didn't tell me about it, I wouldn't have to face it. I declined as politely as I could, and dared not wonder if I'd ever be forced to change my mind.

Tony's illness became more severe; as things moved from worse to unbearable, we opted to have hospice care at home, and we tried our best to live our life together as normally as we could.

And in July of 2001, a little more than two months before Tony died, I called Lynn and invited her to tea. "If you're still willing, I'm ready to talk about the end of it," I said, my voice catching in my throat.

Lynn came to tea. We sat at the dining room table in the house we had found together almost two years before. My hands shook as I poured.

Tony came into the dining room from his office, and sat cheerfully at the table. He had decided that he wanted to hear it, too. If Lynn found this disconcerting, she never said so. She's a hell of a woman; she is also far more courageous than I am.

I asked her many questions, haltingly at first, but then, as Lynn got specific about her life and her experiences, I calmed down and my questions became more purposeful. Tony asked a few questions, too, but generally he was quiet, listening as he studied Lynn with sympathy and respect shining in his big brown eyes.

Lynn calmly sipped her tea and told us about the death of her first husband, in the hospital. She sipped more tea and told us about the death of her second husband, at home. She spoke easily enough; the talk did not break her, even as my own tears fell. She was more focused on soothing my anxiety, and Tony's too, than she was in testing the depths and limits of her own pain. She was candid and genuinely light-hearted about the harsh, cold facts, telling me things similar to what you probably already know from your own journey from active, loving partnership to solitude.

What matters the most here is that she told me: "Imagining how it's going to be and being afraid of what's going to happen, is often actually worse than the way it will play out."

I wasn't so sure about that. But I chose to trust her wisdom and experience, and to take her at her word.

Her word was true.

Tony's journey toward the completion of his life was difficult and unpleasant and agonizing for both of us, on so many levels. But the very end of his life, that last day, was so much less horrible than I'd feared it was going to be that I can smile softly about the final pieces of it even now.

I nearly missed the blessing that is Lynn in my need to control the energy around me and also act as a safeguard for her. It might have been the right motivation on my part, perhaps, but it would have been definitely the wrong move. Because Lynn was and is so generous of spirit, and chose to share the painful stories that were part of her experience with cancer and with the loss of beloved husbands, she helped to make my own journey a bit less awful. Her example inspires me to share my surviving-the-loss-of-Tony episodes with others who may need to hear them, in the hope that someone else's terrible journey can be made a touch less so because I am willing, like Lynn, to talk about what I have lived through, and to carry some helpful, hopeful light into sometimes dark and disconsolate places.

Fear of the process of death is a natural reaction, but Lynn taught me that I could choose to *not* be afraid. She showed me that I had many choices in what seemed at first to me to be a cruel series of completely untenable, devastating circumstances.

What Lynn has also taught me is that there is a stunning potential for joy and happiness in the world, even after being widowed twice. She has the facility to open herself up to life, to laughter and to love; two years ago, she married for the third time.

The last time I talked with her (a week ago, no kidding) she was happy and well, very much in love, and is shining in her work as a realtor.

She continues to inspire me to stay open to life's unexpected blessings.

Famous Last Words

I DON'T KNOW FOR SURE when it first occurred to Tony that he would, at some point, have the opportunity to speak his last words. I could tell, though, that by the time he got around to talking about it with me, he had been thinking about it for some time.

You have to understand that Tony was related to a show business family; Vaudeville, film, professional theater and personal drama were in his blood. He didn't take the acting path that some other members of his family did. He was a pretty good actor in his way, and had the looks for it, but he was cursed with (or blessed with, depending on your point of view) a terrible memory and so would never have remembered his lines if he'd gone pro. Instead, Tony followed his heart and went into the technical side of show business, and was an accomplished makeup designer, puppeteer, sculptor and special effects technician for both stage and screen production. He had a strange and abiding gift for and love of building intricate miniatures, space stations and buildings and mountain ranges, which he often did for fun when he wasn't doing it for movies. He worked in the film industry in Los Angeles for a long time before I met him, and when together we finally moved out of LA for greener pastures, he continued to work in films and commercials for a handful of years.

He'd come by the theatrical side of his nature honestly enough. And we had to admit that his cancer continually added a touch of the dramatic to our world, whether we liked it or not.

So it was no surprise to me that he'd been thinking about his own final conversations with his family, his friends, and his wife. It was, however, quietly disconcerting to me that the man who actively preferred complete denial with respect to his illness and his approaching death would talk openly with me about his thoughts on his last words.

"I think," he said, a little more seriously than I was comfortable with, "that I'd like to do the 'White Plume' speech from the end of *Cyrano de Bergerac*."

What?

I knew he had always loved the play by Edmond Rostand. When he was feeling badly depressed or terribly unwell, he would slide the Jose Ferrer version of *Cyrano* into the VCR and lose himself in it for the duration. He didn't do it often, maybe six times in as many years, but when he sat down and watched *Cyrano* alone, I knew he was in a difficult and miserable place. I also knew that *Cyrano* would make him feel better.

"Yeah," he said, nodding his head with conviction. "I'll do the 'White Plume' speech! It'll be brilliant!" It was one of his favorite soliloquies. "Not a dry eye in the house," he added with a satisfied smirk.

I couldn't help it; I bit my lip until it hurt. I clenched my teeth together and tried not to smile. Then I burst out laughing, and couldn't stop.

"What's so funny?" he demanded, indignant that I was having this much fun at his expense when he was so earnest about it all.

There was no graceful way around it; I had to ask, even though I knew the answer: "Sweetie, do you even *know* the 'White Plume' speech?"

He had to admit that he didn't know it by heart. He had the content, of course, but not the exact beautiful words.

"Sweetie," I continued carefully, making best efforts to smother another fit of giggles, "this would mean that you'd have to memorize it. Pretty soon."

He gave me a regal look; much dignity shone in his brown eyes. "I could memorize it."

"No, you probably couldn't, Hon."

"Why not?"

I shook my head at him, still grinning. "Tony, what did you have for breakfast this morning?"

His dignity was slipping ever so slightly; his eyebrows raised and lowered like busy drawbridges as he tried to remember but couldn't, quite. "That's not the point," he said stubbornly. "That was breakfast. *This* is art!"

He never did memorize the damned speech, although it's become one that I quietly cherish, partly because it's beautifully and touchingly written, a little because it was so appropriate for Tony and his own perceptions of his situation, and mostly because he loved it so very much.

Undaunted, Tony went in search of some meaningful words with which to bring down the curtain on his life. I thought this was a little strange, but I'd been learning to honor his processes, and to tell the truth, this was one of the easier of his strange notions I had to deal with. Still, I couldn't help poking fun and getting in his way just enough to keep the conversation lively.

We watched "Monty Python and the Holy Grail" for the 429th time, and we got to the part where the Knights of the Round Table happen upon the cave where, carved on a wall, are "the last words of Joseph of Arimathaea: 'He who is valiant and pure of spirit may find the Holy Grail in the castle of aaaaaaaaaaaaaarrrrrrgh...."

"You know," I chuckled as I poked Tony in the ribs playfully, "In the scheme of things, that's probably going to be a lot closer to the way you will play your exit. I can't imagine you'll have much time to do anything, um, *prepared*."

"You have no sense of style," he said crossly. "I don't think I'll talk to *you* at all that last day."

"Fair enough," I retorted. "At least I won't have to be checking text to make sure you got the lines right."

A week or so later I was in a shop at the mall and found a pack of cards called "R.I.P: Famous Last Words, A Knowledge Cards™ Deck of Great Exit Lines." I bought them. I took them home, wrapped them in bright red tissue paper, and gave them to Tony over dinner.

He was thrilled. We had a blast looking at what other people had (allegedly) said right before they died.

Here are some of our favorites:

"I've just had eighteen straight whiskies. I think that's the record." (Dylan Thomas)

"They couldn't hit an elephant at this dist—" (General John Sedgwick, Civil War hero, right before the sharpshooter got him.)

"Either this wallpaper goes, or I do." (Oscar Wilde)

"On the whole, I'd rather be in Philadelphia." (W. C. Fields)

Tony finally abandoned the effort to come up with something meaningful to say at the end of his life. He figured that as long as his last words weren't "I've fallen and I can't get up!" or the less complicated but fully sincere "OUCH!," he'd be all right.

I don't know exactly what he said to his family when he talked to them on the phone the last time, about two weeks before he died. I went into another room and gave him the privacy he needed to say what he wanted to say. All I know is that he closed the book with his family in such a way that he was either satisfied or at least at peace.

I also couldn't tell you what he said to most people the last times he saw them; I can only acknowledge that he never said goodbye to anyone. That wasn't his style. I think he carried on, tired as he was, as though he'd see everyone later, like next week, maybe. That was the way he wanted it. It was the way we all wanted it, too.

Tony's last actual conversation with me, which happened about thirty-six hours before he died, went something like this:

He was sitting on the couch in the living room. He hadn't eaten for a couple of days, and it was obvious that he was feeling fragile and disoriented. He was more troubled than I'd seen him in weeks. I knew his body felt lousy.

"What's the matter, Sweetheart?" I asked lightly, wondering if I really wanted to know, but asking anyway.

He looked at me hard. "I'm thinking that you're going to send me to the hospital to die."

This startled me, since it had never been a possibility as far as I had been concerned (and I didn't know that he'd be leaving me so soon). "I think you've got that all wrong, Babe," I reassured him honestly. "Remember I promised you a long time ago that that wouldn't happen, no matter what? And didn't you just hear me arrange for the hospital bed to arrive tomorrow morning, so you'll be more comfortable when you are lying down?"

Suspicious and perplexed, he nodded his head gravely, studying me as he tried to remember if he'd heard anything about the bed or not. "Really?"

"Yep," I said, sitting beside him and taking his hand into my own. "I'm the most practical person in your world. Would I have [illegible] d for you if I wasn't absolutely going to keep [illegible] me?"

[illegible] onceded, eyeing me steadily as he tried to [illegible] ing the truth. After a long minute he took a [illegible] mself relax a little.

[illegible] ked.

[illegible] said. "Sorry. You aren't going to send me [illegible] iistaken."

[illegible] said.

After this, he slept for the rest of the day. The following morning, before the hospital bed arrived, he faded gently into the gray area between unconsciousness and coma.

On his last full day of life, he didn't talk, he simply acknowledged the people around him by opening his eyes momentarily and mustering a faint, abstracted smile at some of the things that were whispered in his vicinity.

By the evening, he was taking small and tentative trips out of his body. It was very like Tony to want to test the water before he jumped all the way into it.

And his last words? I'm not going to tell you what he said. Tony said them to me and to me alone. I doubt they would have much meaning to anyone else.

The moment could not have been better or more natural; his last words were spontaneous, matter-of-fact, and from his heart. He could not have planned them; neither of us could have predicted what I would say to him in exasperation in the last hours before he died that would prompt him to utter the two small words that underscored our life together so peacefully. In that moment he wasn't connected to his body enough to hand me something canned and theatrical, although I know he'd have dearly loved to have been able to still channel Cyrano. Somewhere out there he's shaking his head and grinning, because he's finally come up with a way that he might have been able to pull off delivering that speech with style and a certain panache.

With those two tiny words he gave me the sweetest reassurance about how he felt about me and about all of our years together. His (for me) Famous Last Words were a precious, priceless gift that loss and time and distance and even the possibility of a whole new life can never take away.

But that's not what I meant to tell you.

What I meant to tell you is that I find myself thinking about my own last words. Not the ones I'll cleverly utter at the end of my life so much as the ones I just said to Duncan when he walked across my desk and stood on the keyboard as I write this. I gave him a sudden verbal staccato of annoyance (and entertainment at the same time—he is actually a very cute cat), a little sharper than he deserved, a little more animated than I expected.

I'm thinking of the power of words, how comforting and affirming were the words Tony gave me at the very end, how much energy and purpose lives in the words we use daily and what we do with them to either encourage or injure the people around us, or even ourselves.

Tony used to get frustrated when I'd bellow at rude or crackbrained drivers on the road. "You of all people should understand the power of words!" he would tell me repeatedly. "Why would you put that much negativity into the air?" Then he'd smile and say "It's not like they could hear you anyway, so you've generated all kinds of negative energy even though the words got wasted."

This did not prevent me from having a few choice and largely unwasted ones to give to him, but I did get his point. The trick was coming to terms with my irritation at idiot drivers, and I've gotten better about that over the years, just as a matter of discipline.

I'm trying to be mindful, too, about the words I *don't* say. One of my friends has a set of criteria against which she measures many if not most of her words: *is it honest, is it kind, and is it necessary*? I have seen her in action: if she doesn't feel that a comment she is about to make fits all three elements, she often elects to keep her mouth shut, leaving words unspoken.

I admit that I bristle at the notion of weighing words this carefully; the free (and somewhat cranky) spirit in me prefers to let my words loose at will and let heads fall where they may. But I'm thinking that my friend might be on to something here.

In the odd moment, it might be nice to know that my last words to anyone on any given day would leave them feeling as good, as loved and as appreciated as Tony's very last words left me.

Reruns

IF YOU MISS YOUR FAVORITE television program, kids, don't worry, there are always reruns. In the generation before VCRs, this was one of the first things I learned as a small child from my father, who loved to watch television; reruns were a good thing, because they could "catch you up" on stuff you missed for whatever reason the first time around.

Dad was an aerospace engineer, an extremely intelligent, sharp-witted, articulate man who had mathematical equations pulsing through his veins. Most people who encountered him liked him very much. On the plus side, he was rational, analytical, and the owner and operator of a vast, desert-dry sense of humor. He was, for good or ill, the center of my universe for the first eighteen years of my life. On the other hand, he was emotionally unavailable to everyone, including my mother. His example taught me early on to frown deprecatingly at sentiment, sensitivity, and openly expressed feeling, even when those feelings were my own (little did he realize that he had fathered a moody and hypersensitive artist).

We were very much alike, Dad and I, but we could never quite get on the same page. This frustrated us both into varying levels of irritation (his) and tears (mine). I have come to understand that he was in fact as emotional as I am, but he was never comfortable showing it, or acknowledging it to himself.

Nevertheless, he was the first man I ever loved. Predictably, I measured every man I met against him and generally found them sorely lacking. He was the standard I held myself to as well, and we both knew as I struggled to grow up that I didn't quite hit the mark. It is hard to say which of us was the more disappointed, my logical, too-rational Dad or me, his volatile, emotional child. Such is one familiar facet of the uneasy relationship of some fathers and daughters.

At seventeen I left home for college, and then built my life a continent away, rarely returning for visits. I married Tony and settled down into my own safe, happy little world.

When he was fifty-three, my father was diagnosed with terminal lung cancer.

I was badly frightened by the news; I was still blissfully three and a half years from the knowledge that Tony would be fighting cancer as well. (It surprises me, even as I write this, that there truly was a time in my life with Tony that didn't have anything at all to do with cancer on a daily basis. Sometimes it's hard to remember who I was then.) Dad's father and his brother had died of cancer; still Dad was valiant in his resolve to fight and beat the thing.

He dealt with the realities of his illness in typically-Dad ways. He kept on smoking cigarettes (no one but me agreed with him that since the damage was irreversibly done, why should he stop now?). He continued to work. He did chemo, losing his hair but keeping his characteristic sense of humor. He never got emotional about it, at least, not with me. He moved through his illness with a very Dad-like attitude: *Things are what they are; what are you going to do?*

Living across the country, I made weekly phone calls to check in and see how he was doing, what was happening. I did a decent job of not considering what life would be like without him. Instead I plied him with jokes and stories when we talked. We did not speak about endings, and I was good with that.

As far as I knew, from my safe distance, things were "fine" until the day my mother called and told me that she wanted me to come home. Dad was starting to fail; the cancer had moved to his brain. Weary, sick, and no longer able to work in an industry he had loved all of his life, he formally gave up the fight. He only wanted it to be over.

"Come home *now*," my mother said, applying just enough pressure to crack my self-imposed exile from the family. This was going to be an undeniable disaster. I didn't really know my siblings, my mother and I had never really gotten along, and I didn't deal well with sick people. I didn't acknowledge to anyone that I was afraid to see Dad terminally ill. I didn't know what to expect, but I knew that whatever was waiting for me back in Philadelphia wouldn't be good.

Tony couldn't go; he was working on a time-sensitive project that had no wiggle room. I would have to face the family—and Dad—without him. I didn't feel as though I had any choice; I was going to fly across the country and do what my friends unilaterally called "the right thing." It did not feel like the right thing to me, and

I balked at the prospect even as I bitterly resigned myself to it.

I had never played the "family" game well, and had had my share of reasons for keeping my distance. Returning home was not the best way for me to maintain my comfortably aloof posture, but somehow this didn't seem to matter much. I did not want to go back. I did not want to see Dad, but I knew that I should. With a deep sense of foreboding, I told my mother I was on my way.

The good news is that despite the fact that he was so ill, Dad looked very much like Dad when I walked shakily into the family home for the first time in more than a decade. Thinner, certainly, but he looked like Dad. He *wasn't* Dad any longer, though; between the cancer and the medication he was on, the man with the quick wit, the killer sense of humor, and the analytical mind was no longer present. He was Dad on the outside, and a frail and often lost and confused stranger on the inside. There were momentary glimmers of Dad that weekend, stray instances of recognition between us, but those were fleeting and insubstantial.

I hid in the bathroom and wept, battered by the sight of what cancer had done and was doing to my father. It was the cruelest and worst thing I had ever seen.

I did the best I could that first day at home, tried to pay attention to my mother and the whirling activity around my unfamiliar siblings, all the while warily watching over my shoulder to make sure that Dad didn't happen into the room so that I wouldn't have to look at him, acknowledge him or (God forbid) talk to him. And by the end of the eternal, will-this-never-end weekend, if I had not exactly relaxed around Dad, I could at least vaguely participate in helping to take care of him as I tried desperately to function and make sense of the dreadful situation.

Of course I had no idea that it didn't matter if I watched this program or not, whether or not I paid attention.

I blew it. I had failed to consider reruns.

Safely on the plane at the end of the terrible weekend, I mentally shook the dust from my shoes and scrubbed my brain and heart as hard and as thoroughly as I could, erasing much of what I'd seen and felt at my parents' home so I wouldn't have to look at it ever again.

Once back on the West Coast and securely hooked into my own world again, Tony listened as I told him about the things I'd seen and heard, done and said. He held me close and told me that it was all over, I was all right, the terrors of the experience were now in the past, and I was safe.

Of course I believed him. Of course I was safe.

My father died two weeks later, at the age of fifty-four, and a shiny piece of me, along with a shred of my innocence, died with him. I grieved for Dad, but it was a distant, respectful sort of grief, embroidered with small regrets, the wistful acknowledgement of missed moments, and my edgy discomfort in the face of unhappy, inalterable change.

I elected to ignore (and ultimately I forgot) much of my traumatic weekend with Dad, and got back into the business of living my life with Tony.

All was well, for another three and a half years.

I didn't see the reruns coming; once Tony's cancer was diagnosed and I was caught in the initial quicksand with him, I was too busy trying to breathe and cope to think about anything but our immediate survival. And then, despite the sporadic intensity and unrelenting tension of the first nine years of Tony's life with cancer, the brittle memories of that last weekend with my father didn't occur to me. It isn't that I thought they didn't apply: I simply didn't think about them at all.

I asked my mother, the mostly-retired Nightingale, about this not long ago, and she gave me a fair explanation that does much to help me view my feelings from a perspective I can live with.

"The last time you saw your father prior to that weekend was about two years before he got sick. He was still the Dad you knew. When you came home to see him, with no warning at all you were hit in a matter of minutes with the full force of what his illness had done to him, whereas the rest of the family, who saw him daily or weekly, had had a whole year to take in the much slower, smaller changes and assimilate them and cope with them. You got it all at once, and that's hard."

So much for my solid, lifelong conviction that ripping the bandage off fast is always better than the gentle, slow, tentative method. I've learned my lesson: these days I take my time with emotional bandages whenever I can. And I make it a point never to look at the business side of a bandage when I'm done.

The reruns of Dad's illness began for me in earnest that last year of Tony's life. I had no control over them; I didn't even remember that they were there, which seems strange to say, but it's the truth. I didn't connect my feelings about Dad's cancer experience with Tony's at all.

I do now.

As Tony and I traveled down a path that painfully, stealthily intersected with some of the moments I'd experienced with Dad during that much-mudded-over weekend, I began to realize that I wasn't safe from my carefully-banished memories at all. Each and every one of them that I was convinced I'd jettisoned away were present, fully intact in my head, ready to lay waste to me.

They sneaked up on me, insidious and malevolent, magnifying harsh and frightening moments into shrill, anguished despair. I felt not only the fresh, jagged edges of my pain as I tried to cope with a new and alarming Tony issue, but I remembered and relived the forgotten burning ache that had consumed me when I'd had alarmingly similar encounters with Dad.

One night when I was casually and rather mindlessly feeding Tony some vanilla yogurt when he was too tired to feed himself, I flashed on the cherry-vanilla ice cream I had fed to Dad, who had lost his motor skills. Shaken, I dropped the spoon, as if it had been suddenly red-hot in my hand, and startled Tony.

"Honey?" He had a worried look in his eyes.

"It's okay," I reassured him with a forced smile that hid a hollow shudder. "Just reruns."

And it was "just reruns" the day Tony's wedding ring flew off of his finger and hit the floor. Tony's eyes met mine and he knew I was about to either scream or vomit or both. He knew about this one, the one Dad's-Dying-of-Cancer memory that I had never been able to completely push away, the one that gave me nightmares no matter how many times Tony and I had talked about it both before and after he was sick himself.

Dad lost so much weight that my mother wrapped a common, standard finger-sized adhesive bandage around his wedding ring so that he could continue to wear it. As time went on, and Dad lost more weight, more adhesive finger bandages were added. By the time I saw Dad, there were three of them around his wedding ring, and it was still loose. I was horrified, inescapably surrounded, bludgeoned by thoughts and feelings I refused to put into words until I could calmly sort everything out with Tony later. The image of the loose wedding ring haunted me, but I hadn't associated it with Tony and with where he and I were going, until his own ring was too big to stay on his thinning finger.

Tony's mountain of medication was shadowed in my mind by Dad's mound of pills. I heard myself ask Tony (too often) "Are you okay??" with the same guarded note of tension that echoed back at me from thirteen years earlier when I nervously asked Dad the same question. When I watched Tony sleep, toward the end, I could see myself watching Dad sleep, measuring his breaths and wondering what he was dreaming about, just as I measured and wondered about Tony.

I was seeing—and feeling—double. There was a sense of feverish agitation, coupled with an itchy dread I could not easily contain, frosted over with a surreal calm I could not feel. I was hemmed in by the sensation that even the walls and furniture in every room were holding a collective breath and waiting in unholy silence for the end of the world. This hideous perception reproduced itself over and over again as Tony began to move toward his death and Dad moved toward his, the images and feelings and fears mingling, coalescing and fusing in my stomach, in my head, and in what was left of my heart. In a strange way, I was losing both Tony and Dad at the same time: at a dead run, and in reruns.

But that's not what I meant to tell you.

What I meant to tell you is that if I had the opportunity to go back into my past and erase everything I heard and saw and felt that last torturous weekend with my father, I would do it, in a defiant, unflinching heartbeat. The last images I'd have of Dad would be the happy ones I hold closest to my heart, ones I'd never have to rework and juggle into a mentally- and emotionally-safe "cancer free" zone in order to be able to smile. Time has softened my last memories of Dad, eased the edges and harsh colors from some of the internal pictures I carry with me, and I'm good with that. Dad would be, too.

Sometimes I think it will take a lifetime or two to soften up the memories of Tony's long war with his illness, though, and I mutely accept that as part of my world today. I don't have a choice about that, and so I live with it as well as I can.

And if I had the chance to go back and relive Tony's cancer experience with him, it would be a difficult if not impossible choice. There's not a doubt in my mind that I'd want to spend time with Tony, any way I could get him. Yet when I'm brutally honest with myself about it, I'm not so sure I could do it all again, have to learn it all from the beginning, face all of the nasty inevitabilities that colored our struggle with such heavy strokes of heatbreak, pain and utter powerlessness. I don't know that I am strong enough to face the uneasy, ignorant fear inherent in the process a second time, not knowing what was coming, how severely and how quickly it would hit, only that whatever and whenever it was coming, it was unavoidable, and it was going to be bad.

I'd like to tell you that I'm a courageous woman, yet this, the simple hypothetical exercise of considering going back to that time, to be with the man I loved—more than I've ever loved anyone—as he walked those last miles of his journey is enough to make me tremble with remembered anxiety, has me fighting nausea and tears, rage and overwhelming emptiness of spirit.

I'm afraid of the reruns.

No. I probably wouldn't go back and do it again, not even for a precious moment with Tony. Does that mean I didn't love him, don't love him now? No, of course it doesn't. All it means, I think, is that I've finally moved some small distance away from the pain and loss, out of the cold darkness of death's grasp and into the bright warmth of life, for both of us.

Tony's Life After Death

IN THE DAYS AND SOMETIMES weeks immediately following Tony's death, I had to wake up in the mornings and remind myself that he was gone. I even had to ask my friend Shari a few times those first few weeks if he really was dead, if it had truly happened. That's normal in the hazy, surreal world you live in during the initial stages of loss.

It took time, but once I got my head permanently around the concept that he was gone and he was never coming back, I began to be able to learn to be a little less devastated about the eternal separation. And by the time I was genuinely accustomed to the mundane, workaday-world realities that came with having to live without Tony, it was interesting to notice how much time it took the rest of the impersonal world to get with the program.

I like to think of what I call "Tony Non-Sightings" as residuals: unexpected after-images of the man I loved. I admit that in the beginning, I was a little stunned and put off by them, no matter how understandable they were; I allowed the residuals to remind me all over again that he was gone and I was alone. Eventually I let go of that, learned to accept the residuals for what they are, and usually choose to be entertained. Nowadays, the more ironic the Non-Sightings are, the better I like them.

Here's the thing: he was alive for sixty years, so he's going to be getting mail, courtesy of the US Postal Service. Junk mail, mostly, but he's still going to get stuff. I am the one who pulls it out of the mailbox every day, so I had to get used to the idea and not let it get to me.

Now the only thing that sometimes ruffles my proverbial feathers is that some days he gets more—and better—mail than I do.

Tony loved magazines; he subscribed to some pretty expensive ones. I cancelled them all after he died, but he still gets offers for them at a lower cost than the newsstand price, if he'll reconsider and order them again. (I don't think he has done so, since I haven't gotten a bill, but you never know.) I keep hoping the magazines will comp him a couple of their best and most expensive issues, on account of the fact that he's dead and all, but that hasn't happened yet either. Those magazines would look damned good on my coffee table.

The alternative treatment cancer center in our city continued sending him updated research and newsy tidbits for six months after he was gone. He was no longer checking in with them weekly, nor going to see them for his regular appointments, so you would have thought they'd have noticed that something had happened. Maybe they thought he'd been cured (and I suppose that in a way, he was.) But no, Tony's name was on their master mailing list, and it took me too many phone calls to get the nice people at the center to stop sending him their newsletters filled with the latest on possible cancer cures.

In a moment of fragmented defiance aimed pointedly at The Grim Reaper, Tony went a little nuts on Saturday afternoon and joined the Science Fiction Book Club (after an absence of about twenty years) so he could get the ten free books and would only have to pay for the shipping, in exchange for membership.

The books arrived three weeks or so before he died; I don't think he read a single one of them, but I read four or five. Naturally the Book Club wanted him to fulfill his membership obligations (which is only right, I suppose) until I finally made them understand that he was in fact dead and therefore not likely to be able to be an active member in good standing. The Book Club membership evaporated after several attempts on my part to make it go away. And last month, four years down the road, Tony got several pieces of mail from the Science Fiction Book Club, thick envelopes with cheery writing on the front of them: "Tony, we want you back!"

Take a number and stand in line, Book Club. I get first dibs on him.

Oh, The Dead One gets pre-approved credit card offers all the time. Great APRs, too. He can transfer any of his other credit card balances to the new cards, and get 0% interest. Every so often I'm tempted to go for it, just to see what would happen. I could work it out so I'd be entirely debt-free...and the credit card company would have all kinds of fun tracking Old Tony down. It's a thought, anyway.

The medical center where he had all of his surgeries done, where all of his doctors were, and where I spent some of the toughest hours of my life, still sends him requests for charitable contributions for their cancer research foundation. They have fund-raisers, too, that they invite him to attend. I wonder what they would do if he showed up? I'm guessing that as long as he took the checkbook, he'd be welcome. I don't send them money (after all, the request is not addressed to me) but I've made it a habit, when the requests come, to say a quick prayer for the hundreds of people who are currently in need of what the cancer facilities at the medical center provide, and to be thankful for the doctors and the surgeons who did so much for Tony and me during the thick of his battle. They don't really need my money (and quite frankly, over the years I've written enough checks to the medical center for services rendered); these days I'm more interested in sending empathetic, positive energy, and I give that freely.

Telephone solicitors often ask for my Mister. Poor solicitors; I never know quite what I'm going to say until I say it. Depending on my mood, I either tell the pushiest of them politely that Tony's deceased and so cannot come to the phone, or, if they're especially unpleasant, I take them for a little ride that Tony would have absolutely approved of. "No, he's dead, can he call you back?" This is not always nice, but often is kind of satisfying.

I had a lot of fun once explaining to a solicitor from my cellular phone company why it would be pointless for me to get a second cell phone and additional service for my spouse. She was really into her scripted *spiel* and didn't let me get too many words into the transaction, although I'd tried valiantly to let her off the hook.

"Oh, come on, get a cell phone for your husband, go ahead. It'll save you so much money in the long run," she insisted, after I'd politely declined three or four times. "You'll be able to talk to him no matter where he is for a very reasonable monthly fee!"

"Yeah, but the roaming charges would kill me," I predicted cheerfully.

Some of the oddest Tony Non-Sightings involved Caller ID on the telephone. I called one of my friends to ask her something a few days after he died. I noticed that she was slightly distracted for the initial few seconds of the call, and then things were fine. This did not faze me at first, since we were all a little distracted when Tony left.

Eventually I started noticing that no matter who I called, there would be that weird distraction moment, as if the person I was speaking with had to stop for a few seconds and regroup, and then things were okay again.

Weeks later, another friend I called sputtered from the moment he answered the phone. Puzzled, I asked him what was going on. He told me that his Caller ID had indicated that the incoming call was from Tony, and this had, quite frankly, freaked the hell out of him.

I had forgotten that Tony's name, not mine, was on the phone bill, and that our Caller ID was therefore tagged to his name. I thought this was pretty funny, and didn't mind when the phone company took its sweet time in changing the phone billing and thus the Caller ID tagging to my name instead.

I didn't quite understand how people who knew us could tell me that they'd jumped a little, been disconcerted or at least startled by the visual announcement of a phone call from Tony. They knew he was gone, I reasoned, so what was the big deal?

Then one day I was sitting at my desk at work, and my phone rang. I put my hand on the receiver to pick it up, and glanced at the Caller ID.

Okay, I'll tell you the truth. I saw "INCOMING CALL FROM TONY…" and my heart stopped beating for a very long brief instant. It wasn't that I thought it was Tony (it turned out to be a friend who called me at work from my home phone to tell me she was at the house). It startled me; it didn't shatter me, hurt me, or make me sad or uncomfortable. It was weird, but also, somehow, in the back of my heart, I liked it.

He'd only been gone a few months. If he had actually taken the opportunity to call me that day, I wouldn't have minded a bit.

I stopped harassing my friends about getting jolted by potential calls from Tony. And these days, my name is the one that appears on everyone's Caller ID. Things, as they say, are back to normal. What a shame.

Do you think it's bizarre that I find a certain measure of slightly irrational comfort from the knowledge that on someone's mailing list that I haven't yet anticipated, my sweet Tony is still alive and about to get some mail delivered to him at home? Just the thought of it makes me smile.

But that's not what I meant to tell you.

What I meant to tell you is that some of my favorite residuals, those unlooked-for after-images of Tony, have come to me without the ordinary human intervention of not-updated mailing lists and billing information.

In a quiet corner of my life, the energy behind the unspoken longings of my heart, the way my mind plays when no one is looking, and my grudging acknowledgement of my unfinished need for him all work together to provide some of the Non-Sightings that feel, for a fleeting moment, as though he could be present. I no longer look for sweet residuals to show up in my day, but I cherish them when they occur. And they do.

Sometimes, I think, Tony himself provides them; he is with me in the small phantom moments when I'm suddenly aware of him although I haven't been consciously thinking about him. When I encounter anything that generates a vivid reminder of him, whether I'm seeing something he would have liked to have seen, or I stumble upon something he was fond of, or on those occasions when I can hear his voice clearly in my mind, in that instant he is very much alive for me.

It's up to you whether you want to believe that the person you loved and lost can and does manifest himself or herself to you in ways that we're not taught to understand. And it's how you deal with that sweet soul's life after the death that shows you the truth about how you are healing on this side of the fence.

Thank God for Whiners

IT PAINTS THE WRONG PICTURE when I tell you that Tony never complained about the cancer in general, in specific or in the abstract, but it's the truth.

I never heard him bitch about the unfairness of his situation. He did not fuss about how rotten he felt at various stages of his illness. He did not whimper when discomfort or even amplified pain had the upper hand on any given day. He rarely got cranky in the face of post-operative misery and complication, or yell at me too often when I hovered over his long and arduous recovery periods. He refused to protest, remonstrate, grumble, carp, grouch, kvetch or moan and groan about anything remotely connected to his illness, its detection or its myriad treatments. He didn't whine when he was angry about the cosmic cards he'd been dealt (and he *was* angry). He didn't complain when he was frightened about what was happening just then or about what was swiftly sneaking up from behind him (and he *was* frightened). When his body was hurting or he was too tired to breathe or he was falling into yet another non-negotiated alien territory, he never pitched a fit.

I would have, in less than a fast heartbeat. In fact, I did, often, with much blistering vocabulary.

He never complained, and he did not whine, with respect to anything that was remotely linked to his illness. Not once in the ten years he lived with it.

I could have smacked him.

People who knew Tony in those days marvel at his patience with the cancer. They are struck by the way he was somehow quietly resigned to and at peace with the road upon which he found himself. Even those of our friends who understood how fully in denial he was talk about how amazing it is that he didn't mention how badly he was feeling to anyone, as if there had been a marked nobility in staying silent.

Nobility? I find myself laughing with a derisive snort as I consider this. Oh, please.

He truly wanted to keep me from worrying, agonizing and suffering over his private worries and agonies and suffering. By keeping his terror and pain to himself, he actually managed to make it worse for me.

Before his illness, Tony wasn't much of a complainer; however, when the need arose, he was right there with the rest of us mere mortals. When something hurt, he usually said so. He didn't carry on incessantly, or get angry too often, but it was apparent most of the time if something wasn't okay.

Not so, however, after the initial diagnosis of the cancer. It was as though he'd purposely shut down the part of himself that gave him permission to get frustrated and justifiably bellyache about any of it. Even after the second of his five surgeries, although he had already endured more physical suffering than I'd experienced in my entire lifetime, he maintained the immovable stance of seeming to be almost calculatingly, consistently blasé about what his body was doing, whatever that was.

I can see now that the harder he pulled inward to protect me from the things that were frightening him, the further he was inadvertently pushing himself away from me, condemning himself to a deep, internalized cave that I could not reach, let alone enter, to comfort him. He was expecting all along that he would do his suffering, and probably his dying, alone. He seems now, in retrospect, to have been fiercely resigned to that.

I have to remind myself that he, a male raised in the United States in the middle of the twentieth century, had been strongly, irrevocably conditioned to be single-mindedly strong (whatever that really means), to never show emotion, and to never give in to what might be interpreted as weakness. Of course he shut his mouth and kept his fear and misery to himself. Poor Tony never had a chance.

He thought he had the right idea, and I love him for that. But I think he forgot to look at the overall picture; he missed a couple of critical things that needed to be considered before he'd made up his mind. Leave it to my Tony to succeed in doing this, too, the hard way.

Don't think he was entirely consistent in his behavior, though. Late one night in Year One of the cancer saga, one of our cats hurtled into our bedroom, catapulted onto the bed, and suddenly decided to put her brakes on before she slammed into the wall. She used Tony's bare back for her speedway. All these years later I can remember the unguarded, uncensored, and largely blood-curdling shriek that came out of him; I find it a most gratifying memory. The claw marks she left on his back were rather impressive for a short while, and a few of them ultimately left a couple of tiny scars that he could be counted upon to show people for years afterward. "You want to talk about searing pain?" he told them emphatically, winding up for his "The Night Jasmine Nearly Filleted Me" story.

This from the man who balked at and often heatedly refused to show anyone (even doctors, sometimes) his far more interesting scar that ran from hip to hip which, by anyone's standards, had far better stories attached to it.

Serious cat scratches, to be sure. But *cat scratches*, as opposed to *cancer*? Go figure.

And then there's, well, *me*. I have been known to complain at the drop of an aspirin; I like to think it's part of my charm. You never need to spend any time at all wondering if I've got a sinus headache (I probably do); I'll mention it at some point in the conversation. I whine about hangovers, I moan over upset stomachs, I growl about my allergies (believe it or not, I'm allergic to cats). I have been known to grouse about paper cuts. Cat scratches I don't mind, because I feel like they're just part of my territory. Yet if I work out too hard at the gym and pull a muscle I didn't know I had, you'll probably hear about it over lunch. I won't make you insane with the talk about it, but chances are very good that I'll mention it once. That way, at least, you'll know why I'm walking funny.

I have it on good authority that I'm not a hypochondriac (who has time for that?). But I do not hesitate to roll my eyes and groan fetchingly if I'm not feeling well. I don't make you wonder.

You should be delighted about that.

I whined privately, to only my closest friends, as Tony moved perceptibly away from his position as my highly-decorative-yet-functional spousal unit and into the shadows of the disease that uncompromisingly bled his life away. I never complained to Tony himself about how his changes were becoming my changes, and how badly I missed the people we had been before our unhappy introduction to cancer; even at my most self-involved I could not have made myself do that. I carried my complaints silently, until I could bear the weight of them no longer, and then vented them in the presence of people to whom I could speak my painful truths. To only a few folk were revealed the bitter practicalities of my situation:

"I don't know why he's still here...he should have died weeks ago," and

"I wish I hadn't promised to keep him at home, he really needs to be in the hospital to get better care," and

"Sometimes I hate him for being this sick and leaving me to handle everything in our lives."

Most of my friends provided a safe haven for me to whimper and moan and bitch about things that I don't like to cop to, even now.

One time I whimpered bitterly to one of my then-closest friends about how awful it had been to have to take care of him after a particularly difficult episode. I bared my heart and told her my truth, and was surprised to find that she was not only horrified by my bitchy admission, but that she was "disappointed" in me and in how "unloving" I was to have ever had (much less verbalized) the thoughts and feelings that I'd shared with her.

No amount of explanation pacified her; she was convinced that I was failing Tony in the worse possible ways, parading a disloyalty she found, frankly, appalling. After that I learned quickly to be very careful about complaining even in places I felt I had safety and acceptance and understanding.

That said, I still understood the value of getting much of the frustrated-wife, failing-caregiver, spoiled-child kvetching off my chest. And I was sure Tony never heard about it from anyone; no one to whom I whined and vented would have been willing to say anything to him that they thought might hurt him in any way.

And something faintly amusing crosses my mind in this moment, as I think back and remember how we were in those days. Since (during that last year when things got and stayed somewhere Beyond Bad) I didn't complain directly to Tony about any of the unrelenting terrors that were feeding on my heart, I wonder now if it's remotely possible that, since he never actually heard me do it, he believed that ***I*** never complained? Was I strangely heroic in his eyes the way he is, now, in mine?

No. Never mind. It was just a thought.

I've had a lot of time to ponder and, yes, to complain about, Tony's unwavering refusal to complain. And I've decided that while I think I understand his slightly warped reasoning, I'm having a hard time accepting his motives and his perspective while continuing to honor and respect his process.

He came from a family of disturbed (rather than merely dysfunctional), highly-negatively-charged individuals. Too many things that happened in and to his family from the time he was a child were emotionally overloaded. His entire nuclear family was a total disaster about to erupt and take with it as many innocent bystanders as possible. From the time he was little, Tony didn't have much of a chance of emotional survival. He fought unresolved battles from his childhood right up until he died.

As Tony grew up, he never wanted to be part of the family's frenetic, manic energy about even the smallest inconveniences of everyday living. Instead, he schooled himself early on to shut up about anything that might possibly set a match to any given situation, light it into a conflagration that would put him into an uncomfortable limelight. He didn't want to clean up any more emotional toxic waste sites, so he stayed as far away from conflict and negative emotional expression as he could. He was fine with what he saw as positive emotion: love, friendship, affection and the like. The other stuff he put into his art, and dealt with it quietly, on his own sometimes broken terms.

He recognized that when cancer became a permanent part of our lives, we couldn't do much to alter its course apart from attempting to slow it down. The news wasn't going to get any better; it became easier and safer for him to ignore it for as long as he could. We couldn't fix it, he reasoned, so we might as well just try to move far enough away from it that it would perhaps leave us alone for a while. He opted not to talk about it, not even with me.

I'm working to find room for a little entertainment about his silence, and while it still annoys me, I think I've found a streak of ironic fun in it. I'm willing to bet that he made a weird game out of not complaining about the cancer. He had a huge capacity for patience; did he have a long-standing bet with himself to see if he could manage to never whine about anything? Did he rely on the irritation factor it would cause me, since he knew that I have no problem whining when I want to? I'm beginning to wonder if he didn't get a nasty little thrill from knowing without a shred of doubt that I'd always remember that he never made a fuss, no matter what, even though no one on the planet would have blamed him if he had. A Superman of Silence? A Hercules of Inner (Defiant) Control?

Somewhere, he is wearing a smug grin. The bastard.

The only time he came close to complaining was the hideous night he was having such severe chest pain that we both thought he was having a fatal heart attack. (He wasn't, it was just another fun episode underwritten by the damage the cancer was doing to his poor body.) While we waited for the hospice night nurse to get to the house at some really dumb hour of the night/morning, he said to me through clenched teeth, "You know, this is kind of bad." No drama, no tension, no play for sympathy: a simple, quiet statement of fact. That he'd said anything at all was enough to scare the breath out of me. The stiff-upper-lip understatement crushed my heart; I knew we were in trouble in that moment and, obviously, so did he.

Here's my problem with his refusal to complain: too many times, in Tony's self-imposed need to keep things calm and level, he kept his mouth shut when he should have opened it to tell me what was going on. By not telling me when something felt more wrong than usual, or that pain was building, or that he felt very ill or strange and couldn't breathe or swallow or whatever the trip was, things would seem (from my external perspective) to go to hell without warning. Often the event ended up being far more stressful to deal with than if he had just opened his mouth four hours earlier and told me there might be a problem. His waiting until a problem was finally obvious to me after he'd kept it quiet for too long caused him more difficulty, and was ultimately much harder on me, because we were suddenly submerged in crisis mode when the problem might have been less stressful for both of us had it been dealt with earlier on.

I never could get him to see it this way. He had himself thoroughly, stubbornly convinced that if he didn't mention the problem, it would simply dissolve, no matter how many times he had been proven wrong about that. So it didn't help that I had to watch him that much more closely, ask him many more specific questions, and then second-guess the sweet bastard so that I could attempt to navigate us through and past whatever was coming next. By not allowing himself to complain even a little, by never whining despite its utter appropriateness, he refused to participate; his refusal made the process a good deal more difficult than it needed to be.

I know that he genuinely did not want to be a burden or a problem. He did not want to cause me any extra worry or anxiety, so he kept his peace. In keeping his peace, in some ways he was a heavier burden and a more pressing problem, and often caused me greater worry and deeper anxiety.

He never did get the hang of it.

Neither did I.

But that's not what I meant to tell you.

What I meant to tell you is that taking a little time to complain about pain or fear or the broken washing machine or the fact that the cable company kept you on hold for forty minutes this morning can be a good thing. For God's sake, if something is rattling you, *say something*. Sometimes life just sucks, and I don't see anything wrong with recognizing that, and making the effort to point it out on occasion. Personally, I tend to go for loud rather than long, but any way that works for you is a great way to start. And if no one is there to listen, write it in your journal, or tell your cat, or post it on the bathroom mirror until you feel better.

It's okay to complain about stuff you don't like. It's okay to not like the stuff that's happening in your day.

As a direct result of Tony's never complaining and thereby keeping me too much in the dark about the pending horrors that cancer visited on us, I don't easily trust anything or take anyone at face value. I'm forever watching for hidden agendas, subtle half-truths and hellacious subterfuge. And I'm very hard on my friends when they don't tell me how something really is without my having to probe and sense and wonder and worry.

This is one of the down sides of having lived through the experience of losing Tony; I am forever marked by the consequences of his need to stay silent in the face of calamity rather than calling it what it was and then dealing with it. The aftershocks come more slowly now, four years after his death, but they still come, and they still make me uneasy.

When it comes to conversational complaints and related wallowing from my friends, I'd rather someone told me too much, whined too long and loudly about something that's bothering him, complained about something that hurts or scares her. When I've had enough, I can always tell either him or her (with infinite courtesy and tact, of course) to shut up. I've gotten very good about making it known that when I'm done, I'm done. It seems to me a much safer, saner route than facing a stony, valiant silence and wondering when the roof is going to cave in and crush us all.

Note to myself: Forgive Tony for not complaining; he can figure that one out next time. Get over feeling a little badly about complaining when I feel like it; I'll know when too much is too much, and if I don't know, I'm sure one of my friends will tell me. Tony's bothersome sense of graceful nobility, his stubborn denial, and his slightly twisted view of "not being a problem" (although sometimes he was one) died when he did. It's okay to voice unhappy things. It's probably preferable. It's certainly healthier.

Too many of the people working through processes surrounding illness, dying and surviving loss are in dire need of honest, genuine communication. And since illness, death and survival can be difficult to talk about at the best of times, we encounter these things with a severe handicap: we don't want to discuss the issues and the processes and our unrelenting fears. And even if we can get comfortable enough (or uncomfortable enough) to say anything about the illness or the death, we don't always have the words to express what we need to communicate in a situation that is hard to grasp and seems impossible to deal with.

The talking is difficult, of course, and sometimes can be tougher than coping with the physical realities of terminal illness. I tend to be vocal about most things, but even I have moments when I simply can't push the words out to let people know what I need them to know. Without Tony around, I have to work a little more diligently to communicate the things I think are important.

I've come up with an interesting solution: I think I'll find something in each day to bitch about (whether I'm serious or not) just to stay in practice, to keep the communication flowing. And maybe I'll spend a little time perfecting a particularly irritating tone my in whine.

We all should have room to complain and whine and bitch and moan once in a while; it's good for us, and it takes care of us when we need to communicate something but can't quite manage it any other way.

Oh, thank God for whiners: we keep things lively, and you never have to wonder for very long what's on our minds.

Bernie Siegel and Me

ONE OF THE FEW THINGS that I can recall with brilliant, piercing clarity despite the blinding haze of uneasy fear as I sat in the surgical waiting room on the day of Tony's first cancer surgery is the name *Dr. Bernie Siegel.*

I had never heard of Bernie Siegel. There had never been a reason for me to have heard of him before; Tony's dark diagnosis was less than two weeks old by the time he went into surgery.

It was a long day for the surgical team, for me, and for the friends who waited with me. During the seemingly endless fourteen-hour wait, the only one who wasn't sweating that day was Tony. At some point I called Betty. She is my friend/big sister/senior confessor/fairy godmother/surrogate mother/lifelong pal who lives three thousand miles but never more than a heartbeat away from me. I shakily gave her the updated information provided by the surgical team only moments before: things were going about as well as could be expected. Tony still only had about a twenty per cent chance of walking away from the surgery and breathing at the same time. I was exhausted, frightened, and thoroughly unable to focus. Betty asked me a question anyway.

"Have you read *Love, Medicine and Miracles*?" she asked. "It's by Dr. Bernie Siegel."

"No," I said vaguely. What the hell was she talking about? Reading?

Betty is nothing if not persistent. "You should read it. He has another book out, too, called *Peace, Love and Healing*. I think you should get both, and read them. They will help you."

I stared blankly at the buttons on the pay phone. The books would *help* me? Tony was going to die. I didn't need help, I needed nothing short of a miracle. "Sure," I said, suddenly bored and wishing I hadn't called her in the first place. "Whatever."

"I mean it," she pressed. "Bernie can help you."

Yeah, right, I thought. Nothing can help me now. Tony's probably going to die today, my whole life has changed, and she wants me to read a book. Two books. Great.

Betty has known me my whole life; she is not moved when I bristle and grumble. "On second thought," she decided sweetly, "don't go buy the books. I'm going to send my copies to you. Read them, right away. You'll be so glad you did."

I got the miracle I needed; Tony survived that first near-impossible surgery. He also survived the practically requisite post-surgical pneumonia he valiantly battled in intensive care, as well as the bowel obstructions which were an unwelcome but constant companion to that first and then to each of his subsequent surgeries. He even made it through the twelve weeks of recuperation at home, where we first learned that, despite my best and loving intentions, I was not a natural-born, selfless, competent, ever-on-call and cheerful post-op caregiver. During that time we also discovered with some relief that as long as we were both breathing at the same time—and, okay, sometimes shouting—our marriage could safely weather as many storms as the sky dumped on us.

As promised, Betty sent her copies of Bernie's *Love, Medicine and Miracles* and *Peace, Love and Healing*. "Read these now!" commanded the note she sent with the books. "And send them back when you're finished with them!"

I dutifully put the books on the nightstand by my side of the bed.

A week later I tidily put them in the drawer in the nightstand by my side the bed.

The next time I cleaned out the messy drawer in that nightstand, I industriously put the books in one of the many tall piles on my desk in the study.

A few months later, when I finally got around to sorting through the intimidating multiple towers of books and papers on my desk in the study, I found Betty's (well, Bernie's) books and put them safely in the bookcase across the room from my desk.

And I promptly forgot about them.

Tony's second cancer surgery was performed six months after the first one. In some ways it was easier this time. The cancer was back but the tumors were much smaller than before. The surgical team knew us and knew Tony's medical history intimately. The short-term prognosis was technically much better than the initial one had been. The hardest part for both of us was in understanding and accepting that malignant cancer was undeniably, unavoidably part of our reality; we had no room for the safe delusions that Tony's first experience was a one-time thing and that we had safely gotten all the way past it. We had to face the fact that, together, we were living with cancer. Period. I recognized early on that we had a lot of learning to do.

I called Betty and gave her a report on our patient's second cancer procedure from the familiar pay phone in the surgery waiting room.

"Well, thank God you've got Bernie," she said.

"Oops," I said. I assured her that as soon as Tony was home from the hospital, and things settled down, and I had time, I'd read Bernie's books.

"Remember, I want them back," she reminded me.

I promised I'd get them read and returned to her.

Okay, I'll cut to the chase and admit it straight out: it took me a year from the time of the first surgery to read Bernie's books. But I (much like Bernie, as it turns out) am very aware of the blessings inherent in timing issues and the energy behind them. I was supposed to read *Love, Medicine and Miracles* at exactly the time I finally did. (So *there*, Betty.)

It was as clear to me then as it is today that at the precise moment I finally (and yes, grudgingly) opened *Love, Medicine and Miracles*, I was ready to listen, to hear, and to learn.

Bernie and his book changed my life.

I have never actually met Bernie, but after I read his book, I felt as though he was someone I'd very much like to know. His approach was gentle and welcoming; he made me feel like it was okay to peek into *Love, Medicine and Miracles* and see what he had to say about some of the experiences I was struggling with.

When I thought I didn't want to read any more, because I didn't like what he was telling me about my own situation (and he was always on point with it, having had so much more experience with cancer and other terminal illnesses than I ever will), he kindly showed me that I had a lot to learn if Tony and I were going to successfully navigate the scary story we were lost in.

Bernie is very open about himself and what moves him and makes him tick. That was the first thing that drew me into his book. He didn't come across as coolly crisp and unapproachably professional, as had nearly every doctor I'd ever known in my life, both before and after our cancer experience. Bernie chooses first and foremost to be caring and personal, kind and empathetic; he elects to care. He blends his extensive medical and surgical knowledge with reasonable human emotion, truth, a listening ear, and hugs. Reading his book made me willing to think about cancer and death. Bernie helped me to laugh, to allow myself to cry, and ultimately to resolve to accept our situation daily, hourly if need be. Bernie almost seemed to be moving through the worst days of our process with us; he was not about to leave me stranded alone in the dark.

It was as if, from my initial encounter with his books, Bernie entirely understood what we were dealing with. He didn't take the Standard Medical Professional stance we were already accustomed to; instead, he showed that he understood, was sincerely sorry about our circumstances, and was ready to offer his experience and wisdom if I thought it would help.

He helped at once. In a single page, he described too many facets of Tony's personality, characteristics of an individual who would most likely end up with the challenge of living with terminal illness. Bernie was the first person to explain the mind/body connection and *dis*ease in a way that made sense to me in a context that I could relate to personally. It was slowly dawning on me that Bernie knew what he was talking about, and that I was about to learn more about terminal illness and coping with it than I could possibly want to.

Reading those two books was a relief for me as well as a kind of initiation into grief. Bernie didn't pull any unfair punches; he was honest, straightforward, and agreed that the journey we found ourselves on was going to be difficult. I did a lot of crying during that first time through the books; he had some sad stories to tell. He didn't sugar-coat and therefore minimize the impact of what he had experienced and heard from terminal patients and their families. A lot of what he wrote was heartbreaking to the extent that I had to put the book down for a few days and pick it back up when my heart was once again steady enough to face stories of the suffering of other people. Although I didn't recognize it at first, the stories Bernie told gave me the courage to look at my own fears.

One of the best things Bernie's books did for me was to point out that daily encounters with Tony's illness could be meaningful for both of us, and that as we moved through the various phases of the process, we would be able to make use of whatever meaning we attached to it. As a result, Tony and I chose to own our situation, each in our individual ways, certainly sometimes more effectively than at other times, but own it we did. And the active owning of it strengthened our marriage, our friendship, and our resolve to survive as long and as well as we dared.

After thoroughly taking Bernie's words to heart, I saw that even after a fast and nasty year into the cancer process, I was changing. I had learned to see our situation in new ways that never would have occurred to me without Bernie's unique influence.

Thanks to Bernie's encouraging suggestions about reaching out to our medical team, I got into the habit of hugging Tony's doctors. They were stunned and not terribly comfortable with it at first, but I didn't give up. I'm a tactile person; still, I understand boundaries and was very aware that the uneasy Dr. K (family doctor) and the rigid, almost militarily precise Dr. T (the amazing surgeon) were not wild about hugging the wives of their patients. But once I was committed to touching them, nothing stopped me. Wouldn't you know it, in less than a year, I had both (rather uptight) doctors immediately hugging me when we met at the hospital, whether during a scheduled visit or a chance meeting. More than that, they each got into the habit of hugging Tony, too, and I think it was good for all of us. It connected us all in a way the cold, harsh reality of Tony's medical issues did not. Bernie cares as much about helping to reconnect physicians to their patients (and also to reconnect physicians with their own humanity) as he cares about people with life-threatening challenges. Under Bernie's wise and loving mentoring, everyone wins. I like that.

Bernie explained in his books how critical it was for Tony to hear, via audio tape, some guided meditation and some positive, uplifting music during surgical procedures. Tony also needed to hear me telling him to keep his blood pressure down while he was under anesthesia, to keep the bleeding down to a minimum, and to wake up from the surgery hungry and ready to heal.

Game for anything that would do him some good, I made the tape for him the night before his third surgery. Keeping my voice calmly modulated, I told him to stay alive and be well, to ignore what he might hear the surgical team say if it upset him, and to focus on staying connected to his body and taking care of himself. I filled both sides of the tape, and prayed that the music, the meditation, and my emotional support would give Tony an extra measure of help throughout the ten-hour third procedure.

The next morning, I gave the tape, in a small Walkman® with brand-new batteries in it, to Tony before the orderly wheeled him away to the OR. I told the man that Tony absolutely needed to hear the tape during the surgery. The orderly was honest with me: he was not convinced that Dr. T would allow it while he was working; it was not sterile, and it was most likely going to be a nuisance the surgeon didn't want to have to think about. Tony was already stoned on pre-op meds and couldn't press the point, so I insisted as politely as possible that the orderly tell Dr. T that I felt very strongly that this was critical for Tony, and that it was what we both wanted. Shrugging, the man put the Walkman on the gurney beside Tony's hand, and rolled him away.

I heard later that not only had Dr. T allowed Tony to have his tape playing softly on the Walkman during the entire operation, but that when the tape finished on the first side and the Walkman clicked itself off, Dr. T said quietly, "Tony's tape just shut off. Somebody flip it over and hit 'Play', will you? And check his headphones to make sure he's hearing Lisa's voice well enough."

Tony heard the tape continuously throughout the surgery. I hugged Dr. T hard when I thanked him.

Tony's post-operative recovery periods got noticeably easier after that. I'd love to take credit (it was, after all, my voice urging Tony to breathe and relax and connect with energies outside of himself and spend surgery time in a safe and calm place), but I can't do it with a straight face. My friend Dr. Bernie Siegel urged me to do it, and those were *his* words that I read into the cassette recorder for Tony.

Thanks, Bernie. From both of us.

Denial was one of my husband's best and most favorite tools for coping with his cancer, so it took Tony about five years to get around to reading Bernie's books. I bought him his own copies; he read them and made notes in the margins so he could easily find things he wanted to revisit and rethink. He didn't necessarily like everything Bernie had to say. I can't swear that Tony read every page, but when he focused on something he discovered, he paid attention to Bernie's observations and explanations. He was moved by them, and, I believe, comforted in ways I can't begin to measure.

But that's not what I meant to tell you.

What I meant to tell you is that Bernie's books were a perfect safety net that allowed me to make small, frightened steps toward being able to let go of Tony when the time came.

I'd had ten years to get used to the idea (who knew?), but the abstract notion of letting go of the person you love most in the world is very different from the reality. You find yourself standing there at the pivotal moment, holding the hand of your dying partner, realizing that this is the time to do it. You're facing the words you've been dreading, accepting the truth that the words you never thought you'd be able to say to him, ever, have to be said, and said *now*. Tony had to be able to go in peace, had to let go of me as surely as I was trying to let go of him, and he needed my promise that it was okay for him to move away, the reassurance that I would be all right so that he would be free to leave his dying body behind.

Bernie had taught us why this was necessary for both of us. He'd explained it in several different ways, had given examples of how other people had done it, how I could manage it, and why it was the right thing to do to help Tony separate his spirit from his physical self.

As difficult as it was, I was able to let sweet Tony go, in perfect love and perfect trust, because I understood what Bernie had said, and I trusted him, too.

Oh, and I suppose that I should admit to you that I never did give Betty her Bernie books back. They've been in my possession (which, of course, is nine-tenths of the law, right?) for more than a decade now, and I can't see myself giving them back to her anytime soon. I can't quite make myself do it; they've been such a part of my life for so long that I find myself unwilling to let them go. They have her name written in them, probably so I'd remember to send them back to her. No way; I look at her name in black ink on the first page of each of the two books as an added blessing from one of the most important women in my life. I'm holding on to these tired copies of Bernie's books forever.

Newer editions of the books don't appeal to me. The ones Betty sent me so long ago have more meaning for me; my tears fell on their pages. Sometimes the book trembled in my hands as I finished a chapter. A few of the highlighted passages hold great hope and healing for me; they need to be close by in the event that I have to revisit them. Betty's copies of Bernie's books are *my* books now. Who could have guessed that I'd never be finished with them?

I've gotten into the habit of buying *Love, Medicine and Miracles* and *Peace, Love and Healing* for other people whose lives run smack into terminal illness. Bernie, I've probably bought twenty copies of each of your books (not just these two) over the last fourteen years for friends in need, and for friends of friends in need as well. I generally do it anonymously; it's one of the small ways I can help without invading anyone's space. I wrap the books in cheery paper, and send them on their way with a prayer that Bernie will be able to do as much for the recipient —and the recipient's family and friends — as Bernie was able to do for me, and for Tony, too.

Everyone needs to know what Bernie can teach them, because he speaks from his heart and has the ability to touch you where you're hurting the deepest and fearing the most.

Thanks, Bernie. You shared yourself in such loving ways and made the hardest journey of my life survivable somehow, which in my view is nothing short of miraculous. You've also made it easy for me to quietly help others through the simple act of passing your books to them during some of their darkest hours. Because you opened yourself up with love and caring and commitment, you've managed to help us all a find a safe place a little bit closer to the light.

Rings and Things

OVER THE COURSE OF MY twenty-year marriage, I had four wedding rings.

The first is the one Tony slid onto my finger on the day we were married. He made our rings himself; when left to his own devices, my Tony was one hell of an amazing designer. My first wedding ring is a heavy band, made of rose gold, with his name and mine in Runes.

Three months before the wedding, we talked about the design as he developed it. We shared an active love of medieval history, folklore and art, and I watched in fascination as over the next few weeks he deftly reproduced the Runic designs he'd sketched on paper into the solid wax forms that would serve as the original molds for the rings I believed we'd wear for the rest of our lives.

True to form, he worked just slowly enough on each step of the creative process to drive me insane with anxiety. I couldn't see how the rings would be ready for the wedding. He had me try on the wax ring constantly to make sure it would fit and stay comfortable. Time was racing by; the wedding date was getting closer. I began to wonder if we'd have to use the wax castings at the ceremony, and I grumbled a lot.

When he was finally completely happy with the molds (well, as close to completely happy with the finished product as any artist ever is), he handed them over to another artist who worked in fine metalcraft. The metal guy in turn poured fiery liquid rose gold into the molds, finished the rings, and delivered them to us with one whole day to spare. I was too relieved to be exasperated.

We tried our wedding rings on for size, and such was my relief at the fact that Tony had actually managed to get the rings finished in time, and that they both fit, that I burst into tears. Ever oblivious to my total frustration about his timing issues, Tony graciously accepted my tears as applause for the beauty and quality of the rings.

It was right that he did; our rings are absolutely beautiful. There had never been rings quite like these, and there never would be again; they are unique, created by Tony's hands and Tony's heart.

I noticed how heavy my ring was. I hadn't expected that. The ring took up the entire third joint of my finger, and of course it was gold; having dealt with the ring in wax form until now, the final weight of it hadn't occurred to me. (Nor had it occurred to Tony, but he wasn't going to tell me that anytime soon.) His own ring was a bit larger and a bit heavier, but he was a sculptor and had very strong fingers.

"You'll get used to it," he said with that big grin of his that I had fallen in love with in the first place. "Marriage can be a heavy thing."

The next day, at the appropriate moment in the wedding ceremony, my hand in his, he officially slid the beautiful ring onto my finger, and all was well until he let go of my hand. Weighted now, the hand literally fell several inches before I caught myself. And at some point later in the day when I kissed him, I moved my hand to the back of his head, and I inadvertently smacked him hard with the ring. "See?" he moaned plaintively to the wedding guests, "We've been married two hours, and she's already trying to bash my skull in!"

It didn't take long for me to get used to and appreciate the heaviness of the precious art I wore on the third finger of my left hand. I loved it and the man who had placed it there.

Within a couple of months of the wedding, I developed painful blisters under the ring, and my finger swelled alarmingly. It turned out that I was allergic to the copper in the rose gold compound. I refused to take the ring off for several more months, hoping that my body would get used to the copper somehow, but it didn't. So I grudgingly took the ring off and put it in my jewelry box, taking it out every now and again for state occasions, or just when I wanted to look at it. I didn't need to wear a ring to know that I was married, and married to Tony.

My husband rarely took his ring off. He was justifiably proud of it. It had an unanticipated side benefit, too; it was unique enough that it became ready identification for him. Everyone he came in contact with, from bank tellers to film producers, began to recognize it on sight. "Oh, I remember you, you're the one with that ring."

Tony gave me the second wedding ring when we'd been married just over five years. That second one is a simple yellow gold band with five small diamonds set into it.

One evening after dinner he handed me a small, neatly wrapped box.

"What's this?" I asked. It was not our anniversary or my birthday. I opened it, and looked at him, puzzled.

"Do you like it?" he asked me quietly. The look in his eyes held more than just the question, and I tried to figure out what he was thinking without having to ask.

"Yes, it's pretty," I said, and I meant it. I like simple things. "But why did you buy this?"

He shifted uncomfortably beside me on the couch, lips pursed together as he decided how much he was going to tell me.

I spoke Fluent Tony; I knew the look. "Out with it," I commanded gently. "All of it, please."

It took him a little while to tell me the whole story, or what I think is the whole story. The gist of it is this: the company I worked for had had a party a week or so before. We had attended, and had duly mingled with the crowd. And while I was talking to someone several feet away from him, he overheard a slice of conversation coming from a group of women I barely knew. They were talking about me.

"She's *married*?" one of them gaped in genuine surprise. "She's so outspoken. Too opinionated and too forward. So *loud*. So—"

"...so totally unfeminine!" supplied another with a sniff of disapproval.

A third woman offered skeptically, "Are you sure she's married? She doesn't wear a wedding ring..."

This seems to have stunned Tony, which surprised me. By this time he had lived with me for a long while and should have known that, all right, I am somewhat outspoken, modestly opinionated (I have never liked any variation of the concept of "forward" as it is derogatively applied to assertive women). It is true that I have no trouble making myself heard, whether I am growling, shouting or whispering.

But this silly exchange had troubled him, for reasons that were never entirely explained to me. He did not get specific about what bothered him the most about this, and I chose not to press him. I took what he told me as the bottom line. He concluded that yes of course I was married, and that stupid things like what he'd overheard at the party would not be said if in fact I was wearing a wedding ring. He didn't ask me to wear the ring he'd made for the wedding; he did not want my hands discomfited by the allergic reaction. So he sidestepped this dilemma by buying me a new one.

I decided that I liked the little diamonds.

I wore it, to please him. I admit that I prefer white gold to yellow (and I thought he knew that, but evidently not). I did not need a wedding band on my left hand to remind myself (or to announce to the world) that I was married, and that I was married happily to Tony. The wearing of it made him feel better, for his own loving and protective reasons. The troubled look in his eyes faded when I took it out of the box and put it on. Easing his mind, even if it was over something I perceived to be a foolish matter, was worth much to me.

My third wedding ring is a delicate, elegant white gold filigree design topped with a round, deep red garnet centered between two tear-shaped amethysts. Tony surprised me with this one for our thirteenth wedding anniversary. He'd finally got it through his head that I didn't generally wear yellow gold; I wore rings on several fingers in those days, all white gold except for the simple "second" wedding ring. His artistic sense of visual balance must have finally moved him toward my obvious preference.

When I saw the ring in the box, I gasped with delight. I love this ring; it's my favorite of all the ones he ever gave me. It looks faintly medieval, and the colors of the amethyst and garnet suit me, my temperament, and my taste.

He gently tugged the gold band off of my third finger and pushed the new ring on in its place. I wore it constantly for the next five years.

As the years moved along, my body changed with the seasons and also with my levels of stress as his illness made its hugely random impacts on us. On the days when my fingers were fat, I wore the gold band with the small diamonds. On days when my fingers were behaving, I wore the garnet/amethyst ring.

My fourth wedding ring is a plain silver band. I chose it, and bought us each one when Tony's cancer got more aggressive and he started losing weight. He was not happy that his original ring no longer fit him, but he silently resigned himself to yet another unkind, illness-related sacrifice. He knew I would not ever tighten his ring with an adhesive finger bandage. Problem solved: new rings for both of us (his noticeably smaller). I had them inscribed, and the secret of that inscription was precious to him for the rest of his life.

With a heavy sigh he surrendered his original wedding ring; I put it safely away in my jewelry box, where it sat close beside my own original one.

He wore the silver band until a month before he died. I made him take it off when, over dinner one evening, he gestured vigorously with his hand to make a point, and the ring flew from his finger and sailed across the room.

My eyes were wide, but dry. I made best efforts to breathe. "Not good, Honey," I told him. When I retrieved it, I lay it on the table beside his plate.

I was still having nightmares about of my father's wedding ring sadly padded to fit his thinning fingers. Tony knew all about the worst of those bad dreams, since he was the one who woke me when I was whimpering or muttering unhappily in my sleep.

"I guess I've lost more weight than I realized," he conceded softly, with a shrug. "Sorry about that."

He never wore the ring again; instead, he put it on the third finger of my left hand, where it rested just above the one I already wore. We didn't say a word about it; by tacit agreement I wore his ring and mine until he died.

Afterward, I put his silver band in the jewelry box with all the other survivors.

But that's not what I meant to tell you.

What I meant to tell you is about the day I took my silver band off for the very last time.

During the last year or so of Tony's life, my weight ballooned precipitously. I have since learned that this is fairly normal in situations like mine. Not only was I finding whatever temporary comfort and safety I could in food, but I was eating for Tony as well, and as often, as I could. Eventually he couldn't handle the smell of food cooking in the house, so I was living on fast food, stuffing myself with it as I sat in the car before I came into the house.

Months after his death, as the shock of being completely without him began to subside a little, I found myself staring at myself in the full-length mirror in my bedroom. I couldn't believe what I saw: a middle-aged, overweight and unaccountably frumpy-looking female (who was starving to death on so many internal levels) who was not very attractive, looked tired, lost and had all but given up. I was staggered by the realization that I had no idea who this woman was. I knew how she felt, though; I could see the pain in her eyes, could read there the horrors of her past, the anguish and loneliness of her present, and the cold uncertainty of her future.

What frightened me more than anything else was the jarring recognition that I didn't remember who she was without Tony around to help define her.

Despite her obvious misery, she was not someone I could put my arms around and comfort, even though I understood just how much she needed to be held.

So I dealt with her in the only way I could then: I refused to look directly at her. I learned to ignore her entirely. Eventually I avoided her completely.

And in the interesting paradox in which we all live, where sadness and grief collide with the need to be practical and the will to survive, I kept myself in motion — frenetically sometimes, and often in the wrong direction, but I kept on moving. I went back to work with a vengeance, seemed to most observers to be handling my stuff well enough, and crawled uneasily back into the circle of life, all the while struggling daily to redefine myself without words like "Tony," "widow," "death," "cancer," "grief," and "loneliness."

I wore my silver wedding ring like a blazing talisman against… against what? It didn't keep me from being bitterly lonely. It didn't save me from the brutal memories of loss and illness and death. It didn't protect me from the deafening silence that shrouded my life; it left me confused and hugely unfocused. I used the ring as an anchor; in the beginning of my healing process I never committed myself to the question of what it was I was anchoring myself *to*. That was too much to ask. I merely allowed myself to be comforted by the solid familiarity of it. In my better moments, it was enough. In my worst moments, it *had* to be enough; I had no other choice.

Slowly, very slowly, nearly a year after Tony's death I began to realize that just as the word "widow" was insidiously sending me messages about my perceptions of myself, I was also using the silver wedding band to telegraph messages to people outside of my private, unhappy world.

"Yes," the ring said to me every time I looked at it, "Yes, despite what you look like now, and how you feel about your ugly and unhappy life in general, somebody has loved you." Uh-oh.

But that wasn't the worst of it. What I discovered I wanted the ring to say to other people, even people I didn't know, was: "She may be fat, she may look like hell, and, yes she's all screwed up but, believe it or not, someone actually *loved* her…"

This realization, when it finally hit and took hold, struck me with hurricane force, outraged lightning slicing my heart and frying it at the same time. I was horrified. I had been force-feeding myself a poisonous, steady diet of negative energy, and had wallowed in it for so long that I had lost the ability to see around, through, or past it.

Jolted into unwilling awareness, I began to cry helplessly. I slipped the silver band from my finger and put it with all the others in my jewelry box, and closed the lid on them with a despairing finality.

It didn't take my friends long to notice that I wasn't wearing a wedding ring. Some commented on it, others didn't. I had no answer for anyone. I didn't want to have to admit out loud how I'd been feeling, what I'd been thinking and what I'd been telling myself. I certainly didn't want anyone to know that I'd begun to believe the things I'd been thinking.

At last, I got down to business and went to work on myself; started losing some of the weight. I paid more attention to the messages I was giving myself, and slowly learned to quiet some of my noisier and less attractive internal demons. I made a point of spending more time with friends and co-workers. I began to relearn myself, and eventually truly understood that I could rewrite myself. I consciously chose to make the journey toward treating myself with the gentleness and kindness that we all deserve.

When Tony had been gone nearly two and a half years, I noticed that I had come back to myself in such a way that I decided that (a) I have a ring that I really love, (b) it's *my* damned finger and I can put anything I want on it, (c) I'm no longer hiding behind the concept of what a wedding ring means to me or might mean to anyone else, and (d) to hell with anyone who gives me a bad time about it.

Today I wear the garnet/amethyst ring on the third finger of my left hand. It makes me happy. It's pretty. Tony bought it for me. All the messaging about the ring is positive, life-affirming and joyful.

All in all, not a bad lesson from rings and things.

Shopping Under Pressure

NEAR THE END OF TONY'S life, I had to come to terms with what I still think is the most difficult reality for the loved ones of a cancer patient to swallow: the fact that most people don't actually die from the cancer itself. They starve to death.

I had done my homework, of course. I knew all along that this is what would probably happen, despite my worst nightmares filled with other, more frightening, what-ifs. Intellectually I understood that Tony would literally starve to death. It would take time, but starve he would, and he would do it in my presence.

Our journey had begun to teach me that I couldn't carry every what-if around with me. The terrible manifestations of my fears about what might eventually happen tomorrow or the next day would have to present themselves in their own time. I didn't have extra energy to take on any imagined or next-in-line worries, and learned, in self-defense, to ignore them until in their turn they were too loud to tune out. I had to consciously select what I would fret about, how long I would agonize before I forced myself to calm down and get back in the game. So I let the horrifying image of the potential for Tony starving to death sit quietly in a deep, unlit corner of my awareness for as long as I possibly could.

Until the time came.

It isn't that I didn't understand the physiological mechanics of the process. Roberta had been very specific about that, having learned early on that for me, information was power, comfort and sanity. I held on tightly to her explanations about what was happening with Tony. Knowing what I should be looking for and paying attention to was the only way I was going to be able to maneuver through the final stages of Tony's life. She sat me down one day, and told me the cold, stark truth. It was staggeringly hard to hear, but I needed the information. She made certain that I understood all of it, and then we never spoke about it again. We didn't need to. It was burned into my mind. It's there still.

Tony wasn't hungry for most of the last six months of his life, but he ate a little at every meal anyway. Partly it was to please me, partly to continue to maintain our fragile pretense that our life was normal, and partly it was because he really liked to eat. As he had more frequent occurrences of bowel obstruction, his enthusiasm for food began to dwindle. Mine did, too, but I found myself eating anyway, out of desperation, sometimes more than making up for what he wasn't eating.

It was not an easy time, but we weathered it as smoothly as we could.

During the last month of Tony's life, he couldn't bear the smell of food cooking at all, which was the first of the signs Roberta had told me to watch for. I remember telling her about it when he could no longer hide the nausea he felt when he caught a whiff of his once-favorite meals being prepared. "It's good you're paying attention," she told me kindly. The beginning of the end had been subtly heralded.

That last month, I lived on fast food or I didn't eat at all. Most of the time, I wasn't hungry.

Neither was Tony.

As his tumors grew, they pressed on all of his vital organs, making breathing difficult, pushing against veins and arteries and thus restricting blood flow and oxygen to his brain, wreaking hellacious havoc just about everywhere. His stomach capacity shriveled to less than a quarter of a cup. It was supposed to play out like this: as he lost interest in food and stopped eating, his internal organs would begin to fail slowly because they weren't getting any nourishment. He would be living on a little water, if and when he wanted it at all. As his organs stopped functioning, he would slow down to the point where he'd be unable to get out of bed. Everything in his body would fail entirely, strained beyond the point of survival. And then he would die.

Cancer is not kind to the body it takes over. I know this, first-hand.

If Tony knew he was going to starve to death, he didn't say so. I never mentioned it to him, either, not during even the worst of my panic-stricken and too-close-to-hysterical moments. I didn't want to own the words, and saying them was not going to do either of us any good, so they went unspoken.

But never unconsidered.

Still, every so often, Tony would get a wild hair, and decide that he was hungry. And when he announced that he wanted something to eat, I charged into action, never caring if it was the middle of the night or if I was on my way to work or had just stepped into the shower. If he wanted to eat, then, by God, I was going to see that he got whatever he wanted. If he wanted to eat, he couldn't be starving to death, could he? And if he wasn't starving to death, our time wasn't running out, was it?

The catch here is that once he wanted to eat, I had to hurry to get him whatever it was he was interested in; if I waited too long, his urge to eat would pass, and it might be a day or two before he wanted anything else. So the clock was ticking from the moment he asked for something.

There was the day he wanted a national brand of frozen French Fries, the kind you either deep-fat fry or bake in your oven. They had never been part of our diet, but if he wanted them, I was determined that he was going to have them.

The grocery store is only five minutes by car from our house; I went to the store and bought him a bag of the fries. He loved them, and got in the habit of eating about a dozen a day. I was delighted. When the bag was empty, and he still liked the idea of eating them every day, I went a little overboard and bought six bags of frozen fries.

He lost interest in them the next day, and never ate another. (I found them in our "extra" freezer when I cleaned it out six months after he died. I kissed one of the bags fondly before I tossed them all out.)

Then Tony decided that he liked (sorry about this) cottage cheese and green grapes. Together. In the same dish. He had a favorite bowl, a green, triangular piece of stoneware that pleased him visually (it's that artist thing, you know). When he felt like it, he'd get himself about a cup of cottage cheese, put it in the bowl, and then drop a handful of green seedless grapes into it. I couldn't watch him eat it, but I applauded the fact that he did, happy that we were still making a respectable show of keeping the inevitable at bay.

At some point in July of Tony's last summer, I had had a miserable day at work; my project was falling apart almost as definitively as my personal world was caving in. I was tired, cranky, and dangerously hormonal. I had a headache that was nastier than I was. Tony had not eaten for two days.

Traffic was terrible all the way home, it was raining hard, and the only way I kept from ramming my car into the morons on the road ahead of me was to sing songs at the literal top of my voice. I was in no mood to do anything but get into the house and hide in the bathtub with a glass of Scotch for the rest of the evening. I would ignore the phone, any company Tony had when I got there, and would even make the cats wait for their dinner until I had been given a chance for a long soak, a long drink, and a long bit of quiet.

When I walked in the door, cold and dripping wet, Tony smiled proudly at me. "I'm hungry!" he announced.

"That's so great!" I exclaimed, applauding him, my personal chaos put instantly on hold. "What can I get for you?"

He beamed. "I'd like mac and cheese with tuna in it."

No problem. Mac and cheese was the only thing I could eat in the house when Tony couldn't bear the odor of anything cooking. It was fast, it was easy, and it didn't have much of a smell unless it was in the bowl in front of you. For that reason, we had half a dozen boxes of it sitting in the kitchen cupboard.

"No problem," I told him. I could get his food, and then head for the bathtub.

I opened the cupboard door, and pulled out a box of mac and cheese. I grabbed the butter and the milk, and put water on for the pasta. I reached for a can of tuna...and there wasn't one.

Dammit.

"Honey," I said gently, walking into the living room to talk to him, where he lay reading on the couch, "we have the mac and cheese, but we're out of tuna. Okay?"

He frowned ever so slightly. "I really wanted the tuna." He gave me a little smile. "Never mind. Don't bother with it." He sent me a little kiss through the air, and went back to his magazine.

There was no way I was not going to jump into the car, dash to the grocery store in the deluge and get him a can of tuna. I would have the pasta cooked and the cheese sauce made and ready, and I'd get the tuna mixed into it and piled on a plate before he got to the point where he couldn't eat. I had time, I was sure of it.

The evils of my day temporarily forgotten, I grabbed my wet coat and my purse, gave Tony a quick kiss and the admonition "Stay hungry, dammit!" and ran out the door.

Both traffic lights were viciously against me, but I kept cool. I pulled into the first parking place I could find (it was dinnertime and the lot was pretty full), sprinted into the grocery store, and headed for the aisle where they kept the tuna. I'd been shopping in this place for two years, and knew it well.

I raced to the section of Aisle Four where they kept the tuna. It wasn't there. I found myself surrounded, unaccountably, by croutons and bacon bits.

The store had been reorganized since I'd been there last, a scant two days before. This was no longer the tuna aisle.

Okay, don't panic, I told myself, taking a deep breath. I had been away from home for maybe seven minutes. I could be out of here and home in seven or eight more, and he'd still be interested in eating. Yeah.

I went in search of the tuna. I have a rational, organized mind most of the time, and I trusted my instincts as I hunted in vain for canned tuna. I was running out of time.

My instincts were wrong. The store hadn't been completely reorganized yet, and even the people who worked there weren't altogether sure of where everything was, but they were consulting maps for me. I asked for help from two different store employees, and each sent me in a different direction, neither of which had resulted in tuna. Tension, anxiety, and aggravation building steadily, I ran up and down the aisles, visually scouring the shelves for illusive cans of tuna which were, unfortunately, not there.

This is not only not fair, I heard myself whimper, *it's just wrong!* I wondered vaguely if I'd said this out loud, then decided I didn't care very much if anyone had heard me or not.

I ran down one more aisle, which put me fairly close to the checkout lines, and still had not found what I was looking for. I began asking other shoppers if they'd seen the new home of the canned tuna. No one had.

And then, exasperated well beyond my capacity to politely maintain the tornadoes inside me, I exploded loudly, concisely, characteristically specific, direct, and to the point:

"WHERE THE HELL IS THE FUCKING TUNA????!!??!?!??"

Whoops.

In a matter of seconds, three store employees in little blue aprons ran to me with cans of tuna: tuna in oil, tuna in water, albacore tuna, cat food tuna. The woman from the fresh fish counter materialized behind me. Several of these startled-looking people had known me casually, since I was a regular customer, but when they converged on the aisle in which I was standing, shaking with frustration, all of them seemed more than a little shocked at the big noise that had momentarily drowned out the store's Musak and silenced almost all conversation in the place.

I didn't take the time to blush or apologize. I grabbed two cans of albacore in water, flew to the express checkout stand, paid the cashier, and darted out of the store.

I ran one of the damned traffic lights.

I sped into my driveway, flew into the house waving the cans of tuna, and then tried to walk nonchalantly past Tony on the couch on my way to the kitchen.

"Still hungry?" I asked hopefully as I mixed slightly overcooked macaroni pasta with the milk, the butter and the now-precious tuna.

"I could eat," Tony chuckled from the living room, using a very good Yiddish accent designed to make me laugh.

"Good, because it'll be ready in a minute. Stay hungry."

"Stop making yourself crazy. I'll eat," he said.

You'd better, I threatened him silently. *I may never be allowed back in that grocery store again.*

A minute and a half later, I successfully had the mac, cheese and tuna in his favorite triangular dish. I juggled that with a small glass of water, a fork and a napkin as I walked into the living room with his dinner. *Crazy person triumphant,* I congratulated myself dizzily.

He looked up from his magazine. He looked faintly pained. "I don't think I can eat, Honey, I'm really sorry," he said sadly, feeling more than a little guilty that I'd gone to the trouble of going to the store in the rain and cooking for him. "Maybe later?" he added hopefully.

There was nothing else I could do. I fed the cats, who were moderately miffed at having to wait for their dinner in the first place, and then took myself to the bathroom, filled the tub, and climbed in with a good book and the glass of Scotch I'd promised myself all day long.

Oh yeah, and with a green, triangle-shaped dish of mac, cheese and tuna.

But that's not what I meant to tell you.

What I meant to tell you is that even though I knew that Tony was going to starve to death, despite the fact that this is the natural way the body ceases the fight, I could not make myself let go. I could not let him starve.

I became secretly obsessed with it. Somehow I got it into my head that if he ate anything at all, even just a spoonful of yogurt, he wasn't *really* starving, and he would be able to stay a little longer. I told myself this in spite of the fact that I understand and believe that energy doesn't die, and that he was simply moving on. I knew that his body was overtired, and his soul was somewhere beyond exhaustion; he needed to get ready to leave.

When you continue to feed a body when it's ready to shut down, you confuse the hell out of it. Tony's body knew exactly what it needed to do, and it was trying to do those things efficiently and effectively. If Roberta had known I was bribing Tony with a spoonful of yogurt a couple of times each day, she would have helped me to see reason and I would have stopped pushing it on him. I saved her, and myself, the trouble; I never told her what I was doing.

So Tony's body is trying to shut down, his spirit is trying to leave, and I'm feeding him about a spoonful of yogurt every day his last three painful, stressful days of life, as it turns out, to make *me* feel better somehow. (I didn't.)

He didn't want the yogurt, but he forced it down to please me. He even thanked me for it, and I shudder now at the enormity of the selfishness of my actions, while at the same time I can fully comprehend my motives and my fragmented feelings. I can forgive myself for putting my fear ahead of his need in that moment; I have to. It's one more of those things that Tony would have so easily understood and just as easily forgiven. He was like that.

Most of the time, though, Tony's needs were my primary consideration as his illness progressed. Without realizing it, I allowed myself to get lost.. I drove my own needs so far into the background that they were all but invisible. Too often I forgot or denied that I needed anything at all. I managed to convince myself that the things I was most afraid of were safely locked away in my head, and that they weren't relevant to anything that was happening to us then. I thought this was the right thing to do, the only thing to do.

I was wrong about that. My unspoken fear of watching Tony starve was strangling me, despite my refusal to acknowledge that. I should have stepped back from the deepest and loudest of my fears, looked at them, confronted them, and shared them with someone else. Tony had always been my first and best choice for this, of course, but it was obvious as he got closer to his own end that he was no longer the right place for me to unload my pain and misery—he was carrying quite enough on his own.

So I didn't talk about it with anyone. I should have told Roberta. She would not have scolded me or made me feel selfish or evil. She would have given me a hug, and then suggested ways for me to cope with my very reasonable anxiety. It would have saved me some blind craziness.

The small amount of yogurt I forced on him didn't make Tony's last days more miserable than they would have been without it. I know that. But it's the principle of the thing that has me thinking about it now.

I knew I was afraid, of so many things. I acknowledged that I was exhausted, angry, perpetually on the razor's edge. I kept my fears and exhaustion and anger and all that anxiety in big piles in my head, and when those piles were at their heaviest, scariest and most threatening, I never (because I was terrified at the notion) took the time or had the energy to look at each of the piles to determine exactly, specifically, precisely what was in them. As a result, I was constantly battered by my own internal stuff, which remained blissfully undefined but very loud, while all the external stuff tied to Tony's illness and death slammed into me every day.

It's no wonder I went a little crazy over the yogurt. It makes sense that I didn't want him to starve, and, since I gave him a spoonful an hour before he went into the coma on that last day, technically (not to put too fine a point on it) he didn't really starve, at least not entirely, by my definition. It's my little delusion, and I can hold on to it with both hands if I want to.

And I kind of do.

The Dead Money

LIVING WITH TONY'S CANCER WASN'T all tears, terror and fury. Sometimes we ignored it for a while, with varying degrees of success. Sometimes we grimly acknowledged it as part of what we were stuck with and thus managed to live around it. And other times, we had a little fun with it. What else were we going to do? Since there were no rule books about how people who were working on dying should behave, we kind of made it up as we went along.

The irreverent illness-inspired nicknames I had for Tony, and that I used with snickering regularity, didn't bother him, nor do they horrify me now. But in retrospect I think that Tony and I startled and occasionally offended other people who overheard them. It doesn't matter what the names were; what matters is that we learned that by calling things precisely what they were, the scary and often devastating issues we were dealing with lost a lot of their power to terrify and/or hurt us. Someone said to me the other day, "I still can't believe you used to call him *that,*" and I said tartly, "I think you're more stunned that he used to *answer* to that!"

No, we didn't play by anyone's rules. We didn't believe there were any, once we'd hit the wall with the realization of what was going to happen to Tony and how I would be impacted by it. And neither of us were sad, easily depressed types by nature. We had to stay playful, and play we did.

Which brings me, somehow, to the strange and moderately creepy topic of life insurance. I almost don't want to admit this to you, because I don't especially want to offend you, but we actually called it "The Dead Money." That's all we ever called it, even when our friends gave us a bad time for doing so, and pointed out that it was, in point of fact, pretty tasteless. (You can imagine what I had to say about that.)

There was a private policy on Tony that we'd put together long before he got sick. And I had a good-sized policy on him through my corporate job. I don't know if other people ever stop and think about what life insurance money really does for you; I only know that I'd paid into both policies for years, and never gave them a second thought, at least not until Tony started to visibly fail, around a year before he died.

In one of those moments when we were surrounded by too much bad news (which I wasn't handling all that well), he made some silly remark about if he was gone, I'd still have The Dead Money. I think I smacked him on the shoulder for that. But he had opened the door on it, and suddenly we had a new topic of discussion at the dinner table.

Our friends thought we had entirely lost our minds this time.

How would we spend it? What were we going to do with the money? I had to keep reminding him that *he* would be doing *nothing* with the money, since in order for me to get it in the first place, he was going to have to not be here. This key factor did not dissuade him in the least from considering the possibilities, and he warmed to the subject with an avaricious glow in his eyes that still makes me chuckle.

"You'll have to spend it on something fun," he said. "Make it something exciting!" he added, "Something that will make you smile every time you look at it or think about it. What about a race horse?"

I rolled my eyes at him. I had not been on a horse since I was a teenager, I wasn't keen on racing, and I could not imagine how much work and stress and expense a horse would be. I pointed this out to him.

He was undaunted, and went in another direction. "Get a boat, then," he suggested dreamily.

I shook my head. I do not swim. I get seasick just watching the water, even in the movies. I would not be getting a boat.

"Invest in an art gallery," he recommended. I glared at him; I knew where he was going with this line of suggestion. My husband the sculptor and I had always had very different ideas about art, and we often argued the merits of our preferences with heated energy. I had my favorite styles and media, and he had his; they rarely had anything at all in common.

"Yeah, you could call the place *Why Is This Art?*--because you *still* don't know when you look at it!" He laughed hard and merrily, with the familiar glimmer of creative condescension that always brought out the Mad-But-Surely-Justified Axe Murderer in me.

"Elitist bastard," I muttered, pointing at him meaningfully.

"Sorry Philistine," he countered, with an imperious sniff.

Tony wanted me to have and spend The Dead Money, and he wanted us to have fun thinking about it. And on our better days, we talked about it, and laughed, and dreamed. He loved to plot how he'd spend the money if our situations were somehow reversed. This never fazed me; he was being practical. Besides, there was much more insurance money on me than there was on him.

He was usually sensitive to where my head was before he launched into one of his sporadic plans for spending the money. He knew how close the conversations bordered on his being gone and my being alone (and, frankly, lost without him) so he was careful about broaching the subject most of the time. When he launched into some new idea for using the money to make my life a full-time party, he presented his latest scheme with a gusto that reminded me all over again that he was completely in denial about the part his illness and death would play in the scenario.

On the harsh days, when he wasn't feeling well, or I wasn't, on the days when I couldn't breathe for the ache in my chest at the thought of losing him, on the days when he was worried about the promise of pain and his own unresolved fears about dying, we moved fast and stayed far away from the talk of life insurance. I didn't want to have to think of anything beyond how we were living in the moment; some of those moments were difficult enough without considering anything else.

Only once, just after a particularly hideous and pain-filled episode in the middle of a very long night, did he look me in the eye tiredly and whisper as good-naturedly as he could manage, "You know, Honey, since I'm worth much more dead than alive, I don't know why we're still doing all this stuff. It hardly seems worth the effort of continuing..."

Too exhausted to find a smile or come up with a spontaneous joke, the anxiety I was carrying over his situation that night was amplified and showed nakedly on my face. He was immediately contrite, and screwed his mouth into a sweet but not terribly innocent smile. "Sorry about that," he said nonchalantly. "I was just thinking about you and that art gallery."

I resisted the urge to smother him with a pillow. I smothered him with kisses instead, and we both felt a little steadier.

Several months before his end, we figured out precisely what we were going to do with The Dead Money. Once we hit on this brilliant idea, we were very excited about it, and there was no turning back. (Was it his idea, or was it mine? It hardly matters now, but I think I can go ahead and take the credit for it, whether that credit belongs to me or not. There's not much Tony can do about it, is there?)

We would use The Dead Money for a thing that would make me the happiest: a new bathroom.

The original bathroom in our house was an ugly, strictly functional, skinny little room, only as wide as the bathtub, and about ten feet long. I hated the damned thing; it was the only room in the house that I'd never been happy about.

I'm very much a bath person; I can take a book into the bathtub and stay there all afternoon. I love the bubbles and the bath gel and the salts, the whole thing, and early on in our marriage Tony learned that if I was having a bad day, or was out of temper or out of synch with the rest of reality, the best thing for me (and often for his own safety and sanity) was for me to have a soak in the tub, with or without company, with or without a cup of tea…you get the idea. Planning a remodel of the bathroom with The Dead Money was an adventure that we had a great deal of fun with.

We bought some books on bathroom design. We went to tile stores and bathroom stores and talked about color and ambience. We pondered floor plans and paint, windows and fixtures. We enjoyed the planning, except for one very small point that caught us uncomfortably by surprise.

In order to do a full remodel on the bathroom, to make it everything we, well, everything *I*, could possibly want in a peaceful retreat (in addition to its obvious functionality) we would have to empty out Tony's study, which was the room next to the very tiny original bathroom, and knock out the wall. His study would then cease to be. We'd theoretically understood that from the beginning, but when it finally began to sink in, when we were playing with measurements and the actual room design, the reality hit us both hard and fast, knocked the laughter out of us, and depressed us considerably.

"I can't believe you're not going to keep my study!" he groaned in something close to despair as the thought, and the realities nestled uncomfortably behind them struck him for the very first time.

I put my arms around him, pressed my face against his, and held on tight. "Do you want me to keep your study?" I asked honestly, stunned that we had walked so blithely down this particular path and straight into the emotional ambush. I was willing to do anything to keep him happy in the face of the inevitability that was surrounding him. "We can put the new bathroom somewhere else," I told him, and I meant it. "Or not do it at all. But we can leave your study as it is, forever."

"Yeah," he told me, and I could feel a grin pulling across his face as he regained his internal balance. "Build a shrine or something in there."

I groaned. "Great idea. We can call it 'More of Tony's Crap Piled in Yet Another Room in the House'."

Humor restored, we laughed, entertainment and relief taking over as we put the plans for the new bathroom safely away in a drawer, and elected to put our energy into other things.

Eight months after Tony died, I decided that I was finally ready to knock out the wall of his study and start on the remodel. I hired a general contractor, and work began on the bathroom that we had spent so much time talking and daydreaming about.

I designed the thing myself, and threw myself headlong into the project. I confess I got a little carried away; right before the construction started, after all the elements had been ordered and received, the astute general contractor realized that in my efforts to create the coolest bathroom retreat around, I had made one significant omission. In my excitement about the skylights and the heated floor and the Jacuzzi tub and the separate shower unit, the vanity counter and the pretty cherry cabinets and soothing lighting, I'd kind of forgotten to pencil in the toilet.

It was too late to get a smaller tub. As a result, the toilet had to be stuffed rather unceremoniously in a corner, and lives too close to the tub by my reckoning. Oh well. I'm not exactly suffering over here.

When the work was all done, and the paint was dry, and everything was ready, my general contractor escorted me formally into the new bathroom and gave me a grand tour. Everything was perfect, exactly as I'd wanted it (okay, except for the toilet screw up).

The last thing she showed me in the finished bathroom was a small surprise that left me both speechless and amused at the same time. On the wall by the bathroom door is a small, subtle, silver plaque with the letters TTMB engraved on it. TTMB stands for "The Tony Memorial Bathroom."

He'd have gotten a kick out of that.

But that's not what I meant to tell you.

What I meant to tell you is that, for all the talking and teasing we'd done about it, one of the hardest things for me was touching The Dead Money (plus the $155 that I got as a Death Benefit from the Social Security Administration) once it arrived from both of the insurance companies.

I didn't want it. I wanted Tony back. It seemed to me to be more than a fair trade. I also wanted *me* back, the version of me who didn't know what it was like to be left cold and sad and alone after the death of my favorite person in the world.

Ten times the amount of The Dead Money, a hundred times that much, couldn't give me back all of the things that I'd lost, not just when Tony died, but from the very first moment that his cancer became a part of our lives.

I thought about giving the money away, but it was too much effort to think about where or to whom I should give it. In a brash and angry moment, I considered simply putting the checks on the wood burning in the fireplace and watching them evaporate into the flames. I was less interested in what the checks could buy, the financial security they quietly offered me, than I was in what those checks had cost me.

Having journeyed out of his body and away from his illness and his death, I knew in my heart that Tony would not have appreciated being traded back to me for The Dead Money. He had worked hard to make sure that I understood that I was supposed to move on as he moved away. I didn't want to show him that I wasn't up to the task of living, although it took me what still seems like a long time to be able to do it with much conviction.

I still want him to be proud of me. It matters.

So I spent The Dead Money, and did the things I wanted to do; I know that I did them with his blessing. And I think I did it right. I was able to be simultaneously practical, sensible, extravagant, adventurous, and also to have a grand time in the process. Everything I acquired (especially The Tony Memorial Bathroom) consistently gives me much pleasure and makes me smile.

And no, there is no boat, no race horse, and, believe me, no art gallery called *Why Is It Art*? There's just me, and a few new treasured toys that never fail to remind me of the life and laughter of the man who loved me.

Commuting With Meat

MEAT LOAF, YEAH, THE SINGER/ACTOR, is one of my very best friends.

Well, okay, all right, he's not really one of my very best friends. I haven't met him (yet). But he might as well be one of my closest buddies. I've spent hundreds of hours with him, and he helped me carry myself through one of the most terrible periods of my life.

It occurs to me now, in ways that I didn't think about while Tony and I fought our battles with his cancer on so many simultaneous fronts, how the back-breaking levels of emotional intensity that surrounded our situation folded stealthily into our everyday life. I knew I felt battered most of the time (by what was actually happening as well as by what was going to happen down the road), but I thought that how I felt was normal in light of the illness itself and the unavoidable conclusion that we were facing.

I rarely, if ever, questioned the fury of emotions I carried that never quite calmed down; I functioned at an unmeasured level of constant agitation that became the way I moved through my life. After a while I was completely unable to center and ground myself. And I stayed blissfully unaware of what I needed, because I was focused on what Tony needed.

It's certainly not wrong, or bad, to live a tremendously emotional life, as long as you know something about balance and can find it once in a while. Standing a safe distance away from that part of my own history, I can see that it's just too damned hard to have to carry a constant whirlwind inside you without a break. It's even worse if you're so accustomed to the intensity of the storms that you don't even realize you're spending all of your time spiraling up and down in them.

It didn't take me long to learn by default to misread all of my inner gauges. Eventually, if I didn't have a crisis to deal with (and God, there were so many, so much of the time), well, then, I wasn't sure I was doing anything right.

The last half-year of Tony's battle with cancer was hard on both of us. He was fighting for his life, and I was fighting to hold everything at home and at work on track while keeping as tight a rein as I could on my galloping fears and my fading sense of myself. I thought I was doing a good thing by learning to keep the worst of my fears and internal struggles out of everyone else's line of sight. Still, some of my closest friends wondered quietly if I was going to implode from the constant stress they could read in me but that I didn't usually acknowledge. In my desperation to keep things manageable, I genuinely believed that I had absolutely everyone fooled.

I am not known for bottling up my emotions, but I never saw the point in a ceaseless stream of words and tears that weren't going to solve or change anything in the first place. So for the most part, with the few notable exceptions of my very closest friends, I swallowed my despair whole; while I choked and strangled on it in private, I spent my energy trying to keep things (and Tony) together.

Add to the emotional craziness this piece of the puzzle: as Tony's story was winding down, I felt as if everyone were watching us (and, when I'm honest, watching me) all the time. And I didn't like it. I knew I was going to make, at best, a series of ungracious missteps, and at worst, a fatal error or two. I was not happy at the prospect of going through the long process of losing Tony while under caring, loving observation.

I wonder now why I was concerned about being judged a failure as a caregiver by our friends: *Is she doing a good job of taking care of him? Does she love him enough to take care of him when she's in over her head? Will she screw this up? How selfish is she, underneath the layers of cool, glib, charming competence?* If our friends weren't judging me (and I can tell you that of course most of them were not), I was certainly judging myself, and found myself lacking in too many ways.

Was I paranoid? Perhaps I was, to a point; Tony's last six months were emotionally strenuous for him, for me, for us as a couple, and for everyone who knew us well. Bless them, our friends wanted to help, and made themselves available when I asked. Many of them wanted to know how he was doing each and every day, most everyone needed to stay in touch, and that was fine. Wasn't it?

Most of the time, Tony didn't think so, although he only told this to me (and maybe to Melissa). He worked very hard to stay fully in denial about his illness and the precious ground he was obviously losing. He did his best to ignore his physical issues and live in spite of them. He tried to absolutely avoid talking about any of it, even with the doctors, his hospice nurses, and with me. He announced over breakfast one morning that his denial was perfectly justified: he hadn't signed up for this, and he wanted no part of it, even as his body continually reproduced the malignant cells that were killing him.

My sweet, sunny Tony would much prefer to talk with you about whatever was happening in your life, how you'd spent your day, what was on your mind, and what you thought about this book, that film, or any political issue or current event. He wanted to try out his latest conspiracy theory on you to see what you had to say about it. Often his illness would only enter the conversation if you brought it up; in that case, he'd open up just a little, and he'd work to make you feel easier about it. And then he'd move on to a different subject.

That being said, it's fair to say that he had everyone fairly well trained. So many of our friends were soothed and calmed by the fact that Tony wasn't interested in making every encounter about him and about how he was feeling; cancer was not a hot topic in his interactions with the people he cared about. He had so many other (in his view, more interesting) things on his mind. And as a direct result of this, nearly everyone who knew us understood that the shortest distance between Tony and any illness-related information of any kind was, in a word, me.

Yeah, me.

Remember me? I was the major breadwinner; also the minor house-keeper; the shuttle service; the awake-and-alert liaison with doctors, hospital, pharmacy and hospice; the cook and most of the kitchen staff; the primary caregiver for Tony as well as for our two cats with kidney disease; and the best friend of the guy with the cancer. More than that, I was the unsettled wife trying desperately to keep her husband's world in fragile balance as his body went through its difficult and seemingly impossible changes. So, naturally, in addition to everything else I was doing as a matter of course, I was also responsible for being Information Central.

Email, phone calls, running into well-meaning folk at the grocery store or in the mall—people cared, and wanted to know how he was doing. It's normal. It's kind. But it's also a heavy burden, and the more talking I did about it, the more questions and concerns I answered, the more reassurances I gave, the more I was smothered by the immensity of the responsibility and the unending misery of dealing with everyone's sense of loss piled heavily on top of my own.

What still tightens my stomach, four years after the fact, is that I knew in some dark corner of my mind that I was being emotionally buried alive, but I didn't have the vaguest sense of what to do about it. It didn't matter that my feelings of internal frenzy never slept, or that I had entirely too much to cope with. The process of Tony's terminal illness had brought me to this place, and I had nowhere else to go.

As deftly as I could, I took on Tony's cocky position of denial so that I wouldn't be able to give myself any room to look at what was happening to the small part of me that fought to stay healthy and unbroken by the weight of the persistent strains that living with cancer put on us.

Yeah, everyone was watching me; it's understandable. Tony and I were among the first in our group of friends, and in the larger group of our acquaintances, to have to deal with the nasty reality of fatal illness and mortality on a daily basis. I was about to be the first person most people in my world knew who had lost a partner.

Everyone was pretty sure about how Tony would cope with his disease and his imminent death: he was ignoring it, smoothly, coolly (and somewhat annoyingly, if you ask me). What no one (including me) was clear on was how I was going to deal with the disaster our lives had become the moment we'd had the surgeon's difficult "I'm so sorry, guys, it's finally inoperable" conversation. And since no one knew what I was going to do, there were a lot of eyes looking my way.

It unnerved me.

If no one is paying any attention to you while you stumble through your day, you find that you don't mind too much if you fall down hard once in a while and skin your knees. And if no one is watching, and you feel the need to sit on the ground and cry for a while because you fell down harder than you thought, and your knees hurt, and you've now got a nasty rip in your jeans and your face is dirty and you're really miserable, you find that it's mostly okay to just sit down and wail, loudly, for a while. I've decided that this is a very good thing.

Conversely, if people are watching you (whether it's because they love you, or because the saga is not unlike the proverbial train wreck that draws the eye even as it wrenches the heart, or because they haven't seen this particular movie before, or because you're so damned interesting most of the time), you find that you are suddenly taking their potential emotional reactions to your own stuff into consideration before you make a single step in any direction. It's not noble; it's a form of self-preservation, a deeply artificial but temporarily effective wall to lean your tired back against for a while. If you don't believe me, try bursting into tears about something: don't just cry, completely lose it. Flood the place, howl, screech, beat your breast, moan, and ask your God (loudly) WHY WHY WHY??? It makes onlookers, even those who love you dearly, terribly uncomfortable.

So I learned a few things very quickly:

I had to stay glib and funny and fierce in the face of terrifying adversity.

I had to allow myself no breakthrough tears, or, at least, not many, and not too often. When you cry, most people freak out and feel helpless, and that only makes matters that much worse for everyone. If you're at all like me, you suddenly feel the need to give them a hug and help them to not be so upset that you're so upset.

I had to maintain a convincing stance of complete defiance in the face of nasty Midnight Runs to the Emergency Room, spontaneous discussions with God on the despicable nature of terminal illness, and stray idiot behaviors from some health care professionals who somehow had less experience with terminal illness and post-surgical complications than I do.

After a while it's pointless to let the backwash of emotions rise to the surface, because nothing's News any more. It's a different day, but it's the same old, tedious story: he's still dying, being too brave by half, and having a rough time; you're still tired; life is still miserable most of the time (you can't beat the prognosis, after all);

Friday is still pizza- and date-night; blah blah blah. It's the same old thing, and even the volatile energies fueling the hardships of the day and the terrors of the sleepless nights are kind of boring after everyone's seen and heard them a couple of dozen times. If you take a minute and think about it, you'll discover that it's boring to you and to the dying guy, too, isn't it? Tony would definitely say so.

The point here is that, even though I had a small, tight handful of close friends with whom I was as open and candid as I could be about most of it most of the time, I pulled my "Of Course I'm Fine and Handling My Stuff Nicely, Thanks" face on so often that over time, it *became* my face. My only face.

I inadvertently left myself no room to breathe.

People who know me well can tell you that I am sometimes considered to be a full plate, even on my best days. Who was going to tell me "Don't cry, everything's going to be all right"? Nobody really wanted to have to deal with a total meltdown from me, or have to listen to the harsher private realities Tony and I were facing, for any length of time. I'm sure of that, because Tony and I didn't especially want to have to deal with meltdowns and realities, either.

As a result of the interminal terminal illness-related stuff I was carrying around, plus the glib exterior that I put on with my Levis every day (and yeah, I did it around Tony, too), to say nothing of the responsibilities of my work life and the rest of it, I spent most of the last six months of Tony's life with my head and heart so tightly and painfully knotted up with bleeding and backed-up emotions that I barely breathed from one thought to the next. And after a while, breathing didn't seem to be that important. Who had the time or the inclination to need oxygen? I was well past the point where I believed that I couldn't go on; I simply went on.

There was no safe emotional release for me anywhere in sight. Personal, internal salvation seemed less and less relevant, and my soul trudged on, limping and suffocating, while I did what needed to be done every day.

This would be a good time to mention that I'd already pulled away from nearly all of my favorite forms of joy once Tony started to fade; music and books were the first things to go. I stubbornly chose to live without music, which from childhood had always played a major, active role in my life. My reasons for avoiding music make no sense to me at all now, but I gave it up with a defiance I usually save for idiots and emergency rooms. I have always been a constant, addicted-to-anything-in-print reader, yet I lost my delight in books. For one thing, for the first time in my life, I didn't have the time to read for pleasure, and for another, I couldn't focus anyway. And how could I dare to attempt to lose myself in a book, to hide from the same cold corner of Hell at Our House that Tony would never be able to successfully escape?

Late one night, in one of my mindless, frenetic hours alone after a particularly unpleasant Midnight Run, I found myself angrily digging around in a box in my office at home, and happened upon a stash of old cassette tapes that I'd loved in happier, brighter days. Irritably, I tossed them aside. A moment later, I picked them up again and looked at them carefully, slowly. A tiny light that had been dampened in my soul flickered faintly back into my awareness. In a flash of something warm and unspoken, I had stumbled on a small but intensely positive way to find and perhaps rebuild some of my emotional balance.

I put one of the cassettes in the player in my car the next morning on the way to work, and cranked up the music to someplace just below Absolutely Deafening. I sang along, soft and tentative at first as I found the way back to my voice, then loud and frenzied and wild, with a desperate abandon that began to slowly smooth out some of the sharper edges and deep cracks in my overtired, fragmented soul. I sang until my throat was raw and aching, my pain trickling wetly down my cheeks. That first day, when I arrived at work nearly spent, I discovered with a grateful grin that I was breathing more deeply at that moment than I had been physically able to for longer than I could remember.

The two albums I'd been catharting to were Meat Loaf's and Jim Steinman's *Bat Out of Hell* and *Bat Out of Hell II (Back Into Hell)*. I fully expect the gods to forever shine good things on Jim Steinman for the manic magic of his music and his consistently mind-blowing, soul-scorching lyrics. And as for Meat Loaf...the passion and energy he put into those songs gave me more than enough emotional space to do what I needed to do to keep on breathing. He gave me a safe place to rest and room to let it all out at the same time.

I hung out with Meat every single day on the drive to work in the mornings, and on the same drive home in the evenings. I sang and I cried and I yelled and I howled and I roared and I screamed with the music. (Thank God for Rock.) I let myself touch all the pain and fear in my life over those twenty-five miles between work and home. That commute was the only space in my day when I was completely alone (except for Meat), and I was able to let myself hurt and love and grieve and hate and feel before I had to put the "Yes, I've Got It Covered" face back on, and thus kept my head and heart as safe and sane as I could make them for another day and night.

I don't even want to ponder what I must have looked like driving on the freeway every day, belting out lyrics from "I Would Do Anything for Love (But I Won't Do That)" and "Everything Louder Than Everything Else." Sometimes I let myself sob with pre-remembered pain through "Heaven Can Wait," playing it over and over again until I felt better. At other times I danced with unrestrained glee in the driver's seat to "You Took The Words Right Out Of My Mouth (Hot Summer Night)" while my car crawled along the I-405 corridor. Meat Loaf and Steinman often had me moving faster than my car did in rush hour. If anyone saw me rocking out in the next lane, I was blissfully unaware of it. Some things are better left unconsidered.

But it's true: Meat Loaf and his wholly passionate, highly emotional and sexually-charged vocal energy articulating Steinman's brilliantly beating heart and bitingly funny mind helped me get through what were undeniably the most difficult six months of my inner life.

I kept the fact of my daily commuter dates with Meat to myself. All anyone knew for sure was that I was, somehow, mysteriously calmer, more centered and better-focused when I got to work in the mornings (albeit a little hoarse, was I catching a cold?) even after some of Tony's worst nights. And I seemed to be far more relaxed and ready to take on the evening's many challenges when I got home from work (albeit a little hoarse, was I catching a cold?).

My salvation was Steinman. And it was Meat. And it was me, too.

It isn't just that I know every note, every word, every nuance, every ache, every irony and every sparkle on those two albums. It's also that, even now, when the first seconds of "Bat Out Of Hell" glimmer into auditory existence anywhere in my vicinity, the smile that sneaks its way onto my face is one that never fails to remind me that I am very much alive, entirely awake, and that I'm endlessly grateful that I have a way to give myself room to navigate and successfully weather the unholy sadness of being a lone survivor.

Thanks, Meat and Jim. I mean it. For the record, I've made it a steady policy over the last few years to always have something from your catalogs in the car. But I can't make myself stray too far from the Bats. (It's a happy habit I'm not likely to break.)

By the way, as an indirect result of having Meat singing Steinman in my car, I rarely get freaked and bent out of shape about the potential nastiness of commuting through the dismal parking lot that is the freeway at rush hour. I don't get too pissed off: I've got Meat.

"On a hot summer night, would you offer your throat to the wolf with the red roses?"

Oh yeah, Meat and Jim, I would, in a graceful heartbeat. I know exactly how to do it now.

But that's not what I meant to tell you.

What I meant to tell you is that I have learned that there's no nobility, no goodness, no happiness and no mental or spiritual health to be had in any of the uneasy layers of bottled-up, self-enforced silence for the sake of sparing the feelings of others. I have a news flash for you: nobody's feelings are going to be spared in the process of the coming loss. Our friends experienced the feelings that they carried, and those feelings belonged to them, not to me. What's funny to me now is that I actually believed I could soften the hurt anyone else was feeling then; I believed I could control how the people who loved us felt about our situation and how they would react to it (but of course I never looked at it quite this way).

If I had the opportunity to undo, or redo, parts of how I played my life out in the tapestry of Tony's last months, one of the sections I'd tear out and re-weave would be the constant, canned, auto-piloted polite lies I told, the ones that I thought were keeping everyone else feeling a safe distance from the horrors we were dealing with. I smiled as I assured everyone that, while Tony was having a hard time, I myself was always fine, thank you very much, all was well, I was coping beautifully, I was strong, I could handle whatever came, you do what you have to do, etc. I would have had an easier journey if I'd allowed myself to look at the person with whom I was speaking and say: "You know what? Tony's illness really sucks, and I'm tired, and I'm miserable, and I'm scared to death and I can't breathe, and even though I know you can't do anything about this, I'm glad I can honestly tell you how our world truly is these days. It sucks."

I believe that the unhappy but honest telling would have eased me a little; just getting the words out would have released some of the emotional pressure that I didn't know how to process by myself. And it might have helped our friends, too, to know how I was genuinely feeling inside, rather than having to deal with an often masked, and in some ways, entirely unapproachable version of me. No one would have marveled at how strong I was during those last months with Tony, because the truth would have been out: I'm not that strong. I just appeared to be, for a terribly long and lonely time.

I made a point of getting rid of the "I'm Fine and Handling My Stuff Nicely, Thanks" face. I don't need it any more. The world is a better place when I don't attempt to look like I have much of a handle on anything.

These days, when you look my way, what you see is all there is. Just me.

Encores

IN THE DAYS IMMEDIATELY FOLLOWING Tony's death, I was certain that he was sticking around somehow, staying close to me, doing whatever he could to try to ease my flash-flooding sorrow. His death and the beginning of my lifelong separation from him were just too hard for me to face.

It is true that as I sobbed myself toward sleep, when I felt most alone and miserable those first empty days and nights, I could sense him nearby, calm and strong and supportive. At intervals I felt certain that he was right beside me, and I found myself crying as much over the raw sadness of being without him as I did over the unmistakable feel of him beside me, present and aware, but forever out of reach.

I was lost, and more emotionally battered and unhappy than I thought anyone could be.

Separate and apart from my pain and numb emptiness over the loss of Tony, I had another life-and-death problem to deal with immediately. Our beloved eldest cat, a twenty-year-old, sweet Russian Blue called GreySmoke, was losing his own battle with terminal illness. He was dying of kidney failure. And our fourteen-year-old black-striped tabby, Jamaika, was in the beginning stages of irreversible kidney disease. Tony and I were owned by four cats, and in sixteen years had never lost one.

Grey had lived with us for twelve of his twenty years. I still maintain that if Grey had been taller, had money, and had been a bit more well-read, I'd have dumped Tony in a neat heartbeat and run off with the sweet boy, who was undeniably the quintessential reincarnation of a feline Cary Grant. He was altogether suave, smooth, gorgeous, classy, and delightfully funny.

Grey deftly exercised his natural charm on our other cats (all female) with varying degrees of success. The ever-imperious Jasmine eyed him menacingly when she wasn't entirely ignoring him, but I suspect they exchanged winks and smiles when I wasn't looking, because she never tried to attack him. Jamaika, under most circumstances the most affectionate and eager-to-please of our brood, hissed at him and stalked Grey (which was often entertaining because she was no hunter, and he was an accomplished one). She was known to sporadically instigate heated arguments with her "brother" that Tony and I were never quite able to understand. Darling, timid Fiona, our rescued feral, absolutely adored him, trusting him in ways that she never could allow herself to trust Tony and me.

After having been noticeably ill for several months, Grey started failing in earnest three weeks before Tony died. I took care of both of them with my characteristic stubborn determination, fueled by fears and miseries that I was not brave enough to name.

Tony often sat on the couch in the living room with Grey in his lap. They had some not-very-quiet discussions about which of them was going to leave first, and which of them would have to meet up with the other, after the fact, and where they might do so. I glowered at him when I overheard the mostly one-sided conversations between them; these amusing little chats were not helping me to cope with the pending loss of either one of them. Still, Tony seemed more settled and balanced after these seemingly casual little talks, and now that I think about it, so did Grey.

Both of them had lost too much weight. Neither of them could eat much; both had trouble keeping food down. Each of them kept his unique and charming sense of humor largely intact throughout his respective illness, too, and I relied upon Tony's smile and Grey's cheerful cat-banter in some of the tougher moments.

The man and his cat slept a great deal those last weeks, often curled up together on the couch or in our bed, and I wondered as I watched them what I was going to do without them.

When I could bear it, Tony and I talked about the loss of Grey. I didn't want to face this unnerving event alone; I wanted Tony with me to help me handle our first cat death. We had never had a cherished pet euthanized before, so I didn't know what to expect. I didn't feel up to handling the process under even the best of circumstances. I needed Tony to take charge of this one, to protect me somehow from what I knew was going to be a sad and painful experience.

Tony didn't want me to have to deal with the upcoming loss of Grey on my own, but he realized that, since he wasn't doing too well himself, he wasn't likely to be of much help to me with Grey's process. More than that, as he assessed and acknowledged his own dwindling energy, he had conflicted feelings about his situation, and Grey's, and mine, too.

After a long, emotional discussion, we decided to stop worrying about it (at least, I promised him I'd *try* to stop worrying about it) and we told each other we'd just have to make best efforts to do whatever we all had to when the time came.

When we talked about the idea of Tony dying, I hated that he was so reasonable about it, almost as much as I hated the fact that he was so often right.

"You won't be alone, Sweetheart," Tony said comfortingly, holding me close. "Either I'll be here to help you when Grey goes, or he'll be here to help you when I go." He winked at me, his mouth tweaked into a very Tony-like wicked grin as he called across the room to Grey, who was watching us from his favorite chair. "So Grey, let's try not to pack it in on the same day, okay? It will make her crazy!" Tony nodded somberly at the Russian Blue, then shrugged as he added, "You know how she gets."

If Grey had had an eyebrow, he'd have raised it at me. It was two against one: I was going to get no real help from either one of them.

As it turned out, Tony died first.

The person in the house who suffered over him as much as I did was Jasmine. I had never seen a cat grieve before; the pain in her eyes and her inability to move mirrored my own. She was as lost without him as I was. We comforted each other as well as we could, and I worried about her as we tried to face each new day that we wouldn't be sharing with the man who had been, in his way, the primary care-giver to both of us.

And even as I struggled to breathe and fought to keep faith with the few broken pieces of my life that still made sense, I agonized over Grey, too, in those first few weeks. He was having more bad days than good. I found myself alternately hurling pointless threats at Tony (whether I felt him in the room or not), and almost in the same breath, I'd beg him to make sure that Grey caught up with him when the tired, sick cat's time came.

Grey stuck close to me, partly because he was feeling so badly and needed to be held, and partly because he wanted to do all he could to comfort me, since I, too, needed to be held. Whenever I found myself sitting in a chair sobbing, or lying in bed staring at the ceiling weighted down by a crushing wave of grief too heavy to do anything about, Grey would settle in beside me, lay a paw on my face, and remind me with a twinkle in his eyes that he was still with me.

"You can't help me cope with this one," I sighed often at him, petting him and giving him a kiss on the head. "I'm on my own here." When I did this, he always snuggled closer, as if to kindly indicate the obvious: he was there, and so were the other three cats. I was not exactly all alone.

"All right, all right," I groaned. He *was* right; I still had the cats, a houseful of them. I also had the responsibility for caring for them, which was the single thing that had consistently gotten me out of bed every morning since Tony died. Had it not been for the fact that they needed to be fed, given fresh water, needed their litter boxes cleaned out, and needed attention and comfort from me, I would have had a far more difficult time staying connected to what was left intact in my world. They were helping me aim for balance, and I knew it. And so, I suspect, did they.

Grey stayed as helpful and present as the other cats, until he began to fade away in earnest.

Seven weeks after Tony's passing, Grey was so ill that I knew it was finally time to make arrangements to set him free. There was no doubt that he was ready to be finished, and I sadly made the appointment with our vet.

On the morning of the appointment, I gave him a little of his favorite food (which was not at all good for cats with advanced kidney disease, but everyone at our house had long since learned the true value of quality of life). I held him, talked to him, told him a few jokes, and even let him "drive" us to the vet's office (because I was in no shape to). I bit my bottom lip hard to maintain my faltering composure. I was still raw and battered over losing Tony, and I knew that if I let myself cry about what was going to happen to Grey before anything actually did happen, I'd never get through it.

Our vet had known Grey from the time he'd first charmed his way into our lives. As Grey's doctor, the vet was sad about the euthanasia but agreed with me that it was time.

Grey's veins were not in great shape, so the vet decided to take Grey out of the examining room we were in, carry him to the back room and put a catheter in Grey's foreleg to make the final shot less painful. Grey was getting a tranquilizer, too (for the record, no one offered me one, and that morning I sure could have used it). The vet told me that he and Grey would be right back, and he closed the door behind him, leaving me standing in there alone.

But I wasn't alone; I knew it in a heartbeat.

As I leaned heavily on the examining table, trembling as I considered what was about to happen to Grey and me, I felt a very familiar energy in the air to my left and a little behind me. I had been around that energy for more than twenty years; I had lived my life around it, slept beside it, loved the man from whom it had emanated.

It was Tony. *Encore!*

There was no question that my husband, who'd been dead for nearly eight weeks, was there in the examining room with me. I would have recognized him anywhere. I didn't turn and look; I didn't have to. He was present, more present in that moment than he had been even in the last week of his illness.

He knew how upset I'd been at the prospect of dealing with euthanizing Grey all alone, and he hadn't let me down.

I kept my eyes focused tightly on the door in front of me from which the vet had just left with Grey. I took a deep breath, and then exhaled slowly. Yep, the energy was still there, and I noticed abstractedly that I was calming down. My body stopped trembling, and I felt a comforting warmth seep over the cold anxiety I'd been carrying all morning.

Did he touch me? I don't know. But I knew inexplicably that he was keenly aware of the situation, and had consciously chosen to be with me, and with Grey at his end.

"Nice of you to show up," I said to Tony steadily, almost but not quite managing my characteristic smart-ass tone. I took another breath. "You know how much I need you here now. Thanks for coming."

The energy moved a little forward, hovering closer behind my left shoulder; it felt warmer, and tingled faintly. I didn't move, but tears welled in my eyes. "Thanks, Honey," I whispered, choking a little.

Seconds later, the vet returned to the room with Grey in his arms. The energy beside me stepped back slightly but I still felt it there, steady, strong, and warm.

Eyes swimming, I kissed Grey, ran my hands tenderly along his thin, tired body, and told him how much Tony and I had loved him, would continue to love him, and that this parting would be hard on me but that it was all right. I reminded Grey gently that he knew just what to do.

I nodded at the vet, who also had tears in his eyes. He administered the shot, said, "Goodbye, Buddy," and Grey relaxed in my arms and in a moment was more peaceful than he'd been in weeks.

Then a beautiful thing happened. As Grey let his last breath out, the vet, who had known Tony and I and all of our cats fairly well over the years, softly said, at the same moment that I said it then: "Go find your Dad."

I closed my eyes, and kissed Grey one last time. As I did it, I felt the unique and cherished energy that was Grey leap lightly past me to a spot just behind my left shoulder.

Suddenly, the energy that had vibrated behind me vanished. I cried hard, then, not so much from the grief, which would come later, but from the purest sense of relief I'd ever experienced. My two beautiful men were gone from me, but I knew without a shred of doubt that they were together, and that made my losses a little easier to bear.

If Jasmine noticed that Grey was gone, I saw no evidence of it; she was distracted, paralyzed in her grief over Tony. Jamaika didn't trust that Grey wasn't lurking somewhere in the house; she spent a few days hunting him, then got bored with it and stopped looking. Poor, lonely Fiona walked through the house calling him.

She searched for him, crying for a week before she got used to the idea that, like Tony, Grey was gone and would not be coming back.

Life moved on, and I started the slow and unsteady process of learning to live without Tony, and without GreySmoke. Some days I did better than others. Time flowed forward, and carried me along with it.

Ten months after Tony died, Jamaika was diagnosed with cancer in addition to her much-progressed kidney disease. Over the next two weeks, she was very ill. The vet and I agreed that it was time to set her free, so I made my second euthanasia appointment in less than a year.

After that, Jamaika had a rough couple of days and, two days before her scheduled euthanasia, she had a massive stroke on the living room floor at my feet.

Frantic, I called a friend who lived close by, explained what was happening, and in minutes he was driving us to a nearby but unfamiliar emergency veterinary clinic.

I talked to Jamaika all the way, babbling as I fought to stay calm and comfort her, but things went from horrible to hideous by the time we got to the vet clinic and into the room where she was immediately, gently euthanized. The vet there told me that Jamaika certainly would have died anyway that morning; we had shaved off maybe ten minutes from the process. But at least it was done, and my beloved cat wasn't afraid or suffering any longer.

The suffering, of course, would be left for me.

And for Jasmine, too, who (at fifteen now) had had Jamaika around to play with for fourteen years and who didn't appreciate major life changes. And for tiny Fiona as well, who had slowly moved her wistful allegiance to Jamaika after Grey died. The sweet feral cat found herself unwittingly abandoned once again.

After Jamaika was taken away by a veterinary technician, I signed the paperwork and paid the bill. I was thoroughly drained, in shock, horrified by the suffering I'd seen in the eyes of the cat that Tony and I had raised together but who had loved me best. Her passage had been much more difficult and frightening than either

Tony's or Grey's. I was sick at heart as my friend put me into his car and drove me home. My arms ached with emptiness.

On the way, he said carefully, "Do you know what you were saying all the way to the emergency clinic?"

I had no idea what he was talking about, and told him so.

He said, "You kept saying, 'Tony, where the hell *are* you?' and 'Tony, you'd damned well better catch her when she comes!'"

I looked at my friend woodenly. I hadn't realized it, but it didn't matter. It didn't surprise me, either.

I was fully aware that I hadn't felt Tony anywhere near Jamaika and me that morning, and it made me sad, and angry too. I've since decided that it's very likely that he did catch Jamaika at the end. Just because I didn't feel him close by the way I did when Grey left doesn't mean he wasn't there for Jamaika. I had recognized his subtle presence fleetingly in the early days after he'd died, and I wondered if, as time moved on, he simply had moved with it. Perhaps that made it more difficult for me to recognize if and when he was around me. It made sense, didn't it? Perhaps he'd made another encore, only I'd missed it.

There's an adage that I like to meditate upon: *As above, so below*. As things are in heaven, so they are on earth; as things are on the one hand, so they are on the other. As things are in life, perhaps so they are in death. I can live with that. In life, Tony was a loving, nurturing, protective steward of his cats. I can't imagine he'd feel any differently about it now, especially since I choose to believe he's got two of them with him these days.

That's the only way I can look at the jagged, gaping holes that the losses of Tony, Grey and Jamaika have left in my heart. Thinking about it this way keeps the sadness manageable.

Tony's encores happen at the strangest, sweetest moments. I think he's finished with what he'd certainly call *Grand Gestures*, as when he joined me at the vet's office with Grey, though.

Some of his smaller encores aren't as clear and definable. Yet every so often I can distinguish a momentary flash of him, of his energy and humor and loving protection, and I know that on some plane I can't quite see, he is very much here. Try as I might to discount it, even in private, I can't help but feel just a little bit safer, a little less alone, and quietly connected to him still.

Not long before he died, we happened to watch the film "Ghost," which we had seen several times before but which had become more interesting to him the closer he got to the end of his life.

We watched the scene where the dead guy runs a single penny up the side of wall to show his living partner that he's there.

"That would be so cool if I could do that," Tony said to me at the time. "I'll have to remember that for when I'm dead."

"Don't waste your time with pennies," I teased him. "If you're going to tamper with physics and money, then use something bigger…like hundred-dollar bills."

"You have no sense of style," he shot back at me with a look of mock disapproval. "Paper doesn't have the same visual effect!"

I shook my head. What was I going to do with him? "At least use something bigger, or worth more…quarters? Dimes? I'm sort of fond of dimes."

"Pennies would be easier to see, don't you think?" he asked with a satisfied grin. "I know you like dimes. But I like pennies." He squeezed my hand. "Yeah, I'll remember that," he added with a nod.

"You're impossible," I groaned at him, and we went back to watching the movie.

He'd been dead for a month, and I was having a terrible day at work. Everything was going wrong; I had had to make a few difficult and unhappy decisions, and I was in a lousy mood. I was not yet out of the habit of needing to tell Tony when things were not good at the office. I reached for the phone on my desk to call him and tell him just how irritated I was when I remembered bitterly for the hundredth time that of course he was gone and I couldn't tell him my troubles any longer. I hated that he wasn't around.

Depressed and growling, I left my office and walked down the hall, past the office of my boss (who is also a friend), and headed for the nearby kitchen to get myself a much-needed cup of tea. As I strode into the room, the first thing I noticed was that the shiny, white kitchen floor had pennies scattered across it. Ten of them; a dime's worth of pennies.

Memory sparked, and my heart began to pound almost painfully. It couldn't be…

I looked around. There was no one else in the kitchen.

The pennies were, it seemed, for me.

Letting out a deep breath, I bent down and picked the pennies up from the floor, and held them tightly in my hand. Tea forgotten, I left the kitchen and went to my boss' office.

I showed her the pennies from the floor in the kitchen. Haltingly, I told her about the stray conversation Tony and I had had about death, pennies and dimes. She had known Tony and his playful humor; now she watched me, wide-eyed.

"Did anyone else know about the conversation?" she asked me in wonder.

"I don't think so," I told her truthfully. I suddenly felt self-conscious and uncomfortable that I'd mentioned the story of the pennies to her at all. Would she think I was wistfully delusional, or that I was losing my mind?

I looked at my boss and tried to find a graceful way to back-pedal from the entire episode. To my surprise, she grinned at me.

"While this may be impressive in its way, I think *you* were right. It would have been much cooler if he'd dropped ten one-hundred-dollar bills on the kitchen floor for you!"

Bravo, Tony. Nice encore.

Not long ago, I was driving on a rainy, wet afternoon and was narrowly missed by an oncoming car that was speeding and went out of control. I saw it coming at me fast, and in the instant that I recognized what was about to happen, my car was forcefully pushed immediately sideways out of the path of certain danger, moved safely out of harm's way by…by nothing at all.

Well, maybe not exactly nothing.

I learn quickly, sometimes. "Wow, Tony," I murmured, stunned. "Thanks."

He would never see himself as a Guardian Angel, nor would I perceive him so or have him characterized as such. His timing wasn't that good, in life.

He'd agree with me about this: by my reckoning, he's just a guy who's keeping the conversation lively with his encore performances.

Tony was very big on collecting quotes he thought were clever or insightful or significant. These he kept in notebooks, sometimes on stray slips of paper that he would tuck away for later consideration. Every once in a while I happen upon one of those small pieces of paper, and find a quotation or note on it, in Tony's easy, comforting handwriting. And wouldn't you know it, the quote I stumble across, more often than not, specifically and directly applies to a problem I'm dealing with, a struggle I'm engaged in, or a moment of pique or indecision I can't get past without help. Coincidence? Maybe.

But I don't think so.

But that's not what I meant to tell you.

What I meant to tell you is that, while I don't know why I bother to do it, I can admit that I spend time pondering the metaphysics of death and the life that surely must extend beyond it. I generally accept that I can't really know what actually happens until I die myself, but I believe that something does happen, of course. And I have unanswerable questions that only spark more unanswerable questions.

Is it easier for those who've died to stay close by us in the early stages than after some time passes? Do they have a chance to come to terms with things and tie off any loose ends that they need to, and then move further away from us as they settle into new, unearthly rhythms and approach the next phases of their existences?

Do our dead people *want* to move away from us after they accept their new situation? Do they not need us any longer, the way we need them? Does their lessened need for us, or our lessened need for them, dictate how active or present they are in our lives?

What is it, precisely, that Time heals?

Is the difference between seven weeks after his death and ten months after his death the reason I knew Tony was there with Grey at the end, but I didn't sense that he was with Jamaika and me that last morning of her life?

What is he doing now? Since energy doesn't die (consult your local physicist if you don't have your head around this), where does it *go*?

Where did Tony go?

And does he love me and miss me, the way I miss him and love him still?

I have to wonder, and wonder I do. I think of him as active, busy, learning and growing, hanging out with old and new friends, and helping others, which was one of the things that made him happiest in life. I also like to imagine him planning his next encore, scheduling it for a moment I'll end up needing it — and him — the most.

On my last day of life, will he be hanging around waiting for me to finish my business so I can catch up with him? I can see him planning his final encore just for me; he'll flash me his wry, familiar grin, take my hand, and say, "There you are! You're late!"

I wouldn't mind at all having it play out that way.

Tony to Ashes, My Heart to Dust

IN DESPERATE DEFIANCE AGAINST EVERYTHING we could think of the night before his very first cancer surgery, Tony and I conceived a slightly crack-brained plan designed to protect our dwindling sense of sanity. We knew that we ultimately would have to do something with his dead body (in the event that he didn't find himself sharing bad jokes with me after a decisive run in the recovery room the next day); we came up with a notion guaranteed to wickedly amuse us, which was all that mattered in the screaming face of the fear we were attempting to outrun.

Solely in the interest of self-entertainment, we decided together that he would be cremated, and that I would then take his ashes (unbelievably called "cremains") to a sculptor, who would mix Tony's bone ash with clay. We would, in effect, turn Tony's cremains into a very attractive weed pot, which would most likely be kept at home, in the living room, near the hearth in front of the fireplace. I would be free to select the style for the pot, and the glaze. He would be free to, well, be the pot.

This idea came very close to horrifying nearly every single person we told. That in itself made the decision a fun one. This got us through the first surgery, each of the subsequent ones, and gave any further talk of death an insubordinate, sometimes blasphemous edge. We liked it that way.

And over the years, we held to the idea that Tony's final form—in death—would be that tasteful weed pot, thus keeping him as functionally ornamental after the fact as before it.

As we got close to the end of his life, we had sporadic conversations about the weed pot. He was still very much in favor of the idea, and I, in the interest of supporting his trip, agreed with him in principle. I also heartily approved of its easy shock value.

"Did you get the names of the sculptors who would deal with the cremains?" he asked me one day. Not *his* cremains, but *the* cremains. He was still in denial, and was making sure that the death part was, at least in the context of the conversation we were having, nothing personal.

I dug through a folder on my desk, and then looked up at him. "Yeah, I've got the list right here," I said, waving a piece of paper at him. "Let me deal with it; let's not make this one of your infamous 'Shop Before You Drop' outings...I don't think I could take it this week," I added, grumbling. Tony had been hitting the mall and the Internet lately as if shopping, instead of Tony himself, was going out of style.

"All right," he conceded gracefully. "Just pick a sculptor you know I'd like talking to, and make sure you like his or her work. And pay attention to the quality...I don't want any flash lines on the pot," he demanded, a prissy *I Am The Artist in This Family and Don't You Forget It!* tone creeping into his voice but remaining mostly unstated.

I smiled sweetly, murmured an expletive that made him laugh, and we changed the subject.

Tony died a month later.

You would have thought that after all the time I'd had to prepare for Tony's passing, it wouldn't have been a shock to me, but it was. At the moment you suddenly tell yourself, "We're really here...he's gone," you're not ready; I'm not all that sure you *can* be. I know that I wasn't. So much for my careful emotional planning.

I sat beside him and talked to his body after he was dead, on the chance that Tony might still be hanging around that morning, keeping an eye on me. I never said goodbye, but I said a lot of other things.

I didn't watch the men from the mortuary take Tony's body away; that would have been too much, and as a favorite friend of mine has said several times over the years, "That's a picture you don't want in your head." I don't have that picture, thank you very much, because of the foresight of the hospice Nightingale and my friend.

So the last time I saw him, he was finally at peace, his body resting quietly in the bed, his hands colder than hands should ever be. They came and took him away, and that was that.

The next day, with Shari and Jane, those two wonderful women I consider closer to me than sisters, I went to the mortuary to take care of all the final stuff.

One of the things that I have noticed about normally competent people who happen to be in shock is that they stubbornly attempt to handle whatever matter needs attention, large or small. They struggle valiantly to force everything to make sense even as it makes no sense at all, calling on a clarity of thought and procedure that has been utterly blown away by the shock itself. What seems like normal, calm, and responsible behavior to the person in shock as she deals with any given issue actually looks and feels a little dicey from the perspective of any onlookers, because it *is*. The person in shock is not firing on all cylinders, but cannot imagine this to be so, which only adds to the surreal nature of the effort.

That's what happened at the mortuary. My sister-friends planned to take care of me when we got there, to help me to make decisions and go through processes that I could not be expected to deal with on my own. They would also provide the emotional support for which they are both famous and well-beloved. With their help, I would be able to almost autopilot through the business of the post-death paperwork.

Unfortunately, although I tried, I could not find my inner cruise control. Instead, I morphed into some strange and creepy combination of *Eerie Super-Rational Woman* and *I Have Been A Professional Paralegal So Don't Screw With Me Today*. I was entirely fixated, it seems, on getting the stuff handled with a cool, competent efficiency that simply was not there under the circumstances. Yikes.

The man handling the business end of Tony's death ushered us into a room and sat with us at a small round table. He opened a file folder, looked things over, and then calmly, quietly and respectfully looked at me.

"You were married to the deceased?" he asked in a low voice, as a matter of form.

No one had ever referred to Tony that way before. I found myself considering this carefully. I'd had many names for him, both sweet and tart, over the course of our relationship, and admittedly I had called him some peculiar and not-terribly PC things during the long run of his illness.

But "*deceased*"?

The string of euphemisms for death from Monty Python's classic "Parrot Sketch" came flooding, unbidden, into my mind, and I couldn't wipe the delirious, hugely-entertained look off of my face for a few moments. (Had he not been busy elsewhere, Tony himself would have been rolling on the floor in helpless laughter.)

"Yes," I choked, trying to stifle a massive case of the chortles as my eyes met the solemnity in his.

"Did you bring his driver's license?" asked the man.

I had. The mortuary attendants who had collected Tony the morning before had made it clear to me that if I did not take his driver's license with its picture ID to this meeting, someone (me? Yikes!) would have to, by law, identify the body. Tony's body. Not something I really wanted to do, even though I knew what he looked like, and I also knew what he looked like dead, having just seen him so not thirty-six hours earlier. Still, no thanks. I handed over the driver's license, someone photocopied it for the record, and it was returned to me. I stuffed it in my pocket without glancing at the familiar face on the front.

Then came the forms and contracts. I don't remember much about them now, but my sister-friends were very careful to make sure that I didn't sign anything that didn't make sense. All the while, I convinced myself that I was reading each piece of paper carefully, especially the fine print. I had been a corporate paralegal for six years, in contract law, and I knew a contract when I saw one, dammit.

I am a fast reader; in defiance of the shock that had numbed my brain, I read every single word on every page.

Ever the professional, I spotted something in the document that required my notice: by signing the contract, I was agreeing to waive a specific right in the event of a technical problem with the mortuary.

"What kind of technical problem?" I asked the man, looking up from the page and meeting his eyes.

"It's okay, just sign it," Jane said. She got it, and didn't want me to go there.

"It's the usual stuff, just do it," Shari said. She got it, and didn't want me to go there.

As is my habit when I'm on to something, I ignored them both and leaned into the issue. "What technical problem?" I asked the man again. "What could go wrong here that you wouldn't want to be held liable for?"

The man frowned. "That's to cover the unlikely possibility that our generator wouldn't function in a power outage."

I didn't understand. I pressed.

"Don't press," Jane said. Jane and Shari got it. They didn't want me to get it, at least not at that moment.

I am nothing if not consistent, even in the hazy realm of shock; I didn't *like* that I didn't get it. I frowned at the man, trying without success to work it out on my own. "Why would you need a generator?"

The man sighed, looked unhappily at Shari and Jane, and gave it up. "To keep the refrigerators running," he said softly.

Refrigerators? What the hell—oh. I got it. And I began to shake.

Tony's body, the one I had loved for so long, the one he'd so recently vacated, was being kept in a refrigerator. The refrigerator's backup support was a generator.

Suddenly chilled to the bone, it was too cold in the room for me to quibble about waiving or not waiving any of my rights. I glanced through the rest of the contract, and mumbled "Just don't let the damned generator die. I don't think I could handle that this week," as I signed the thing. My hands trembled with the cold I imagined Tony was feeling, or, rather, *not* feeling, but that didn't help me much.

The man took the paperwork from me, gave me my copies, and told us that the cremation would occur over the next few days. "They'll call you," he said, but I had stopped listening. I was thinking of my favorite warm body hanging out in a refrigerator, and couldn't get the image out of my head.

The next time I see Tony, he'll be ashes I thought as Shari and Jane walked out of the mortuary on either side of me. Someone would call, tell me Tony was "finished," I would come back to the mortuary to collect him, and this piece of our unhappy adventure could be over.

Afterward, Jane and I went to Shari's house for lunch. I remember warm soup, warm friends, and my agitated wish that

I hadn't pressed about the liability of the generator that kept dead bodies refrigerated. The rest of the day is a blur.

Jane stayed at home with me and the cats for several days, none of which I remember. Shari was never more than a phone call away; I know that but I don't remember anything specific that may have happened between us conversationally. Shock does that. So does exhaustion, fear of being alone when the dust settles, and the uneasiness of wondering what has just happened to you. You can't quite get your head, heart and arms around the idea that the rest of the world keeps on going as if nothing show-stopping has just occurred.

I secretly fed the notion that nearly everyone in the world was insane and sadly disconnected—except me. I knew that life was never going to be the same in a world where Tony no longer laughed. I was frozen in an unwelcoming place where he did not live. He could not love me any more.

Life as I knew it, and as I wanted it to be, was forever changed; I understood that with a miserable, bitter clarity. What the hell was wrong with everyone else?

The day after Jane went home, I was sitting on the couch in my living room trying to remember where I'd put a favorite book of Tony's, when the phone rang.

It was someone from the mortuary. The man was very polite; he said that by law, the mortuary had to let me know that they were about to cremate Tony's body, so that if I wanted to change my mind, I could do it now, or forever hold my peace (or something like that).

The phone trembled violently in my hand, an easy 8.7 on the Richter scale. They were about to do it right now?

RIGHT NOW????

With no breath in my body, as calmly as I could, I told the man that that was fine, to go ahead. It was all he needed from me; I could hang up the phone.

They would be cremating Tony's body right now, **NOW**, and I was fully aware of it and what it meant: Tony was really dead, Tony was really not coming back, and Tony's poor body was about to be...oh sweet GOD why did I have to know that it was happening right this minute?

Shaking violently, spontaneously nauseated and holding on to the kitchen counter desperately for physical support, I immediately dialed Shari's number. She answered the phone at once. Gasping for air, I explained what had just happened. She asked me if I wanted her to come over and be with me. That was all I needed; her willingness to come hold my hand steadied me. I was crying, but I was mostly all right. I told her she didn't need to come, I had only needed someone else besides me to know what was happening to Tony's body (and to my heart). I got off the phone, and struggled unsuccessfully to keep the images of cremation out of my head.

I knew what had to be done next, for myself as much as for Tony. In an instant I was moving more quickly than I had since he'd died. I had no time to lose.

I hurried into the bedroom, and easily found the tall white candle that Aaron and Kim had given Tony for his birthday five months before. Aaron had chosen it at a cathedral in Ireland, and she had had it blessed as a gift for Tony. The minute I saw it after he opened it at his birthday party, and had seen the look in his eyes when he'd thanked her, I knew that it was special, and also that it had one single purpose. When the party was over, I stealthily tucked the candle away in a drawer in the bedroom to wait until it was needed. If he ever wondered what had happened to it, he never asked. I don't know that I could have told him.

In any event, the candle's time had finally come. I took it out of the drawer, and stood it in a simple crystal holder, which I placed on top of the armoire in our bedroom. I said a quick, breathless prayer. When I was done, I dried my tears and reached for a match stick.

"You never liked heat," I said to Tony, who had basked in winter weather but wilted irritably in temperatures above 75 degrees for as long as I'd known him, "but you're getting it now. I hope you got all the way out of your body, Honey, or else you're in for a bitch of an afternoon.

"Go with God, Sweetie," I whispered, lighting the candle. "Tony to ashes, and most of my heart with it, into dust."

I let the candle burn, undisturbed for almost eighteen hours until, just like Tony's life, it burned itself out on its own.

Several days later, the mortuary called and told me that Tony's ashes were ready to be picked up. I called Shari, and we agreed to meet for lunch at a Greek restaurant a short walk from the mortuary before we went together to collect them.

I arrived too early, and waited in uneasy agitation for Shari to show up. I tried to read a book, but could not concentrate on very much for very long, so I gave up. Realizing that Shari was not due to meet me for another twenty minutes, I frowned, then shrugged and got out of the car.

I walked over to the mortuary, and went in the front door alone. I was entirely comfortable with the fact that although I'd been in the place less than a week before, I didn't remember it at all.

I told the receptionist who I was, and what I had come for. She left the room to get the ashes. She came back a few minutes later carrying a square box wrapped in embossed white paper. This she placed on her desk. Then she gave me a form to sign, looked at my driver's license, and finally handed me the box.

I was expecting ashes. As in *fireplace* ashes. As a result, I was not prepared for the surprising weight of the box when she placed it in my hands. Tony weighed a relative ton. I grimaced as I dropped the box on the floor, narrowly missing my foot. It landed with an unfamiliar thud.

The receptionist's eyes flew open, and I had a moment of stark clarity, one of the first I'd had in a couple of weeks: I had just dropped Tony's dead ass on the floor.

I couldn't help myself; I started to laugh. It wasn't that creepy, hysterical, uh-oh-she's-finally-gone-psychopath laughter; it was the easy, ironic, *gotcha* kind of laughter that Tony and I had shared for all of my adult life. Mirth replaced exhausted grief for a few seconds. I found that I could breathe.

Still giggling, I bent down and picked up the box, and apologized to the receptionist (who was as uncomfortable with the droppage as she was with my rippling laughter). I made a stray comment about Tony's compact heft, and walked the box to my car. I placed it on the back seat, and, suddenly hungry, took myself back to the restaurant to wait for Shari.

When she arrived and I told her I'd already picked the ashes up, she said she was proud of me for doing it on my own. When I told her I'd dropped him, she looked at me in typical Shari fashion and said, "Oopsie" and we chuckled and ordered lunch.

It was the very first time I'd been in that restaurant without Tony; he had loved eating there. But he was out of luck this time, and would be from now on. I ordered a bowl of his favorite soup, and ate it in a show of honorable solidarity with him, and in my own self-defense.

In the days that followed, I couldn't pass the dining room table without seeing the square box with the embossed white gift wrap on it. I didn't know where else to put the blasted thing, so it remained on the table. It was not offensive, or frightening; it simply *was*.

It was what was left of Tony.

I found myself talking to the box, but only when no one was looking. I didn't even do it in front of the cats. "You got mail," I'd tell the box furtively when I came in from collecting the daily post, carrying catalogues and magazines with his name on them. "Oh, and I got what looks like four sympathy cards today…but I'm not ready to read them yet, and you aren't going to hear them — anything nice that anyone might have to say about you would only go to your head. I don't think I should have to deal with you smug and dead at the same time!"

Tony's death had occurred three weeks before my birthday. And as people came by to check on me, or to simply hang out, they noticed the pretty box on the dining room table, wrapped in elegant white embossed paper. "Early birthday present?" they inquired politely.

"I think it depends upon how you look at it," I said with a twinkle in my eye.

Some of our friends were startled, some were entertained, some didn't know what to think, most said nothing. The bad news is that I wasn't playing fair. The good news is that no one really expected me to.

After enough comments had been made about my leaving Tony on the dining room table (even when I was serving dinner), I decided it was time to do something else with him. The planned date for his "interment" was a couple of weeks away. I was determined to scatter his ashes in the back yard under the Japanese Lace Maple we'd bought together for our twentieth anniversary. In his present form, he was going to have to hang out somewhere else for a while.

I took the box that held his ashes from the table and put it on the floor next to the bookshelf between the kitchen and the dining room, and left it sitting there for several days. It wasn't a bad place to keep him; placed unceremoniously on the floor, he wouldn't tumble off of anything. It also occurred to me that it might be interesting to keep him at cat's-eye level. He had often wondered what the world might look like at ankle-height, and I reasoned that this certainly would be his final opportunity to look into that. So the box sat silently on the carpet, out of the way of traffic.

Still, something wasn't quite right. I thought about it idly for a day or two, tested my feelings, and decided that my basic problem with the box was that it just didn't feel like Tony. So I went into his office, looked around and triumphantly found the very thing that would make the tasteful yet anonymous box extremely like Tony for me.

From that moment to the night Jane and I scattered him under the tree, the box that held Tony's ashes wore his favorite baseball cap: a black cap with a big picture of his hero, Bugs Bunny, waving a carrot next to the words "What's Up, Doc?"

I liked it. Looking at the box with the cap sitting on it not only made me grin every time I looked at it, but also made him look a little taller. He'd have appreciated that.

Here's the biggest lesson I've learned about dealing with death, with dying people, and with dead people: being alive trumps being dead, every single time. In my view, at the end of the day, or, at the end of the life, it's what the survivors want and can manage to live with that matters, rather than what the soon-to-be- or recently-dead folk want. Not a popular idea, possibly, but one that I hold on to with both hands, regardless of the cost.

A case in point: my beloved grandmother, the only member of my family who ever gave me a nickname and who loved me to pieces long after she gave up trying to understand me, died at the age of eighty. Eighty was all she wanted; it was all she'd planned for. She'd made this clear from the time I was small. I always took her at her word, so her decree was a given, entirely accepted, understood, unquestioned, and certainly unchallenged by me.

Just after her eightieth birthday (which was about two years before Tony got sick), my grandmother called me and announced that when Tony and I came to visit her the following weekend, she had a favor to ask of me.

When Tony and I showed up a couple of hours before dinner on the appointed Saturday night, she sent Tony into her bedroom to rearrange the stuff on her closet shelves so, she said, she could get to things more easily. He cheerfully obliged, and left Gran and me alone to talk.

Then Gran made us some tea, sat down with me and told me that her time was running out, and reminded me about the favor she wanted to ask.

"Are you sick?" I asked, suddenly concerned. She looked and sounded great to me, and at eighty years and one week old had more energy than I did at thirty-four.

"No, I'm not sick, and I'm not kidding. There's something that I want you to do for me." And she proceeded to tell me that she needed me to end my silent feud with her daughter, my aunt, my late father's sister. "I know you don't want to, and I know she drives you as crazy as she makes everyone else, but once I'm gone she won't have anyone else in the family close by. She lives here, you live here. Everyone else is back East. I want you to promise me that you'll make up with her, and that you'll let her make you crazy." My eyes were wide with dull shock. "I don't want her to be lonely; you know she needs someone she can push around, and you're strong enough to take it. Do it for me."

My shock was fading; a rising level of annoyance was taking its place. Despite her generous heart, my aunt was, in so many ways, an insufferable pain in the ass; after a small but intense falling-out, we had not spoken for a couple of years, and to tell the truth I had been the happier for it. "Is this some sort of pre-deathbed request?" I scowled sarcastically.

My grandmother blessed me with the same kind of benevolent smile she'd given me when I was four, the smile that praised *Good Girl! You got it on the first try!* "It is," she said, without apology.

I looked at her; she looked back at me, sure of her victory on this battlefield. I let her have her moment as she poured more tea. She handed me the cup, and I shook my head at her.

"No way," I said firmly.

"What do you *mean* 'no way'?"

I had been stubborn at four years old. I was more stubborn at thirty-four, especially when my sanity was at risk. "Just what I said, Gran. No way."

No way was I going to sidle up to my aunt, no way was I willingly going to subject myself to any unpleasantness that I hadn't rightfully earned, no way was I going to live with the over-manipulative mania that was the mind-bending result of dealing with my father's sister. No way, no matter what.

It was my grandmother's turn to be shocked. "You *can't* say no," she insisted with a touch of pique. "It's my deathbed request."

I aligned my pique with hers; mine was stronger. "I can *so* say no, Gran. NO. I don't know what you've been reading, but just because you're going to die someday..."

"Someday soon," she said gently, with the confidence and resolve I'd admired in her from the moment I was old enough to identify them. "I'm officially eighty, you know. Enough is enough."

"Okay," I muttered, "I get that. You're going someday soon. Your call. But you're not getting away with leaving me with Dear Auntie while you're safely dead someplace and completely out of the line of fire."

"You have to do it. It's a deathbed request, and deathbed requests must be honored."

"Who decided that?" I countered. "Where does it say I have to do something this terrible for the sake of what, a cultural tradition?"

She didn't have an answer for that.

I kept talking; I was on a roll. My voice came quickly, clipped, autumn wind racing through icy trees. "Let's say I'm stupid enough to promise you that I'll play nicely with Auntie, just for the sake of discussion." She eyed me suspiciously. "I keep the promise to you, and I let her make me crazy for the rest of her life, until I have to kill her. Is that what you want?"

Gran nodded. "That's mostly what I'm telling you," she admitted.

I pointed at her with my finger, nearly touching her nose the way she had touched mine when teaching me new things as a child. "You have lost your mind. You've turned eighty and you've gone entirely bats." She opened her mouth to say something, but I glared at her and she closed it again as I hissed, "You want me to give her space to make me insane for the duration. Okay, I get that, it's some weird mother-protecting-wacked-out-child sort of thing. But here's the deal, Gran…I could be a good granddaughter and make you the promise, and I'd be bound by it (by guilt or by stubbornness or maybe an uncharacteristic lack of self-preservation) no matter how much of a continual pain in my ass she'd be, for the rest of her life!" I sat back in my chair and gaped at Gran. "Are you *nuts*? I'd be keeping a promise I should never have made in the first place, and you'd be conveniently dead and have no interest in the evil situation you'd created here. It's really nasty of you to ask that of me.

"If I promised it, solely to keep you happy, I'd end up hating you, too. So I won't promise. I won't even consider it; I will not entertain the notion. Not now, not ever." I narrowed my eyes at her and growled under my breath.

Frustrated, Gran patted my hand. "You won't do it for me?"

"Nope," I told her truthfully. "I have never lied to you. I'm not going to start now. You won't have to worry about Auntie having someone to play with; she'll find someone to torture, trust me. You'll be dead and cheerful, occupied with other more interesting things. I think it kind of sucks that you'd even ask me."

Gran sighed deeply. There was a resignation in the sound that told me that I'd won. Her sigh was enough; I did not have to say anything else.

We stared at each other for a few minutes in silence, and then she squeezed my fingers with her own arthritic ones, which were a more wrinkled, contorted version of mine. "All right," she conceded. "No deathbed requests for you."

"Good," I said.

Her eyes twinkled. "Do you think I could pull this off if I dropped it on your brother?"

But that's not what I meant to tell you.

What I meant to tell you is that Tony never got to be a weed pot.

When I'm honest, I think he'd be a little disappointed by that; he got to a place where he had his mind set on it. He was looking forward, I think, to sitting on the hearth or on the mantle, tastefully glazed, as easy on the eye in death as in life. I could fill him with dried flowers, peacock feathers, whatever pleased me; he was good with that.

However, a couple of months before he died, I'd begun reconsidering said weed pot, but didn't mention it to him; there was no point. I found myself worrying about knocking into the pot with the vacuum cleaner and breaking it, or bumping into it while I was dusting, having the thing which had been part of Tony's body fall and shatter into pieces. I'd have to sweep him up, collect him carefully, and take him back to the potter to break him down to chalk, add him back into more clay, throw him into another pot, maybe a different glaze this time…until I broke him again (I have a sorry tendency to be close by when things break). And then there was always the possibility that I'd get so frustrated with the number of breakages and subsequent reformations that I'd just lose my mind and toss the remaining shards of him in the garbage to end the cycle and get a little peace.

The more I thought about it, the less I liked the idea.

As Tony declined toward his end, I was not interested in acquiring good pottery; I was trying to find air to breathe and ways to cope. It occurred to me in the odd moment that when Tony was done, I wanted him to be *done,* although I didn't define that to myself.

One night after yet another stressful cancer-related adventure, I was wide awake at four a.m., glancing through one of my old journals. On a page written at a time when our relationship was new, I found a quick notation: in the course of one of our initial conversations, Tony had admitted that he thought it would be wonderful to be a tree. He had said that he liked the concept of staying in one place and watching the world move by. He had often thought that he could be wholly at peace with that.

In a flash, I stopped worrying about breaking pottery.

I knew that he wanted to be a weed pot; he knew that I'd agreed to arrange for that to happen once he was gone. It did not, could not, occur to him that I'd do anything other than what he'd said he'd wanted. (Which seems odd to me somehow, because it turns out that while he was rearranging Gran's closet in her bedroom that day, he'd been actively listening to the "deathbed request" conversation. He told me later that he'd agreed with me entirely, and not only because he couldn't bear dealing with Auntie either. From his perspective, guilting people into doing things your way just because you're dying might be great fun in the moment but was ultimately pointless and not terribly fair. And Tony was nothing if not fair, as often as he could manage it.)

But, like I said earlier, being alive trumps being dead, every single blessed time. Gran got the message (I never did deal with Auntie again). And I hope Tony got the message, too. After he was gone I was able to allow myself to gently overrule his well-made plan to be a weed pot, so that I could live in a world where Tony didn't.

This is not to say that I overturned all of Tony's "last wishes;" I didn't. I disposed of most of his things precisely the way he wanted me to: Melissa got most of the art books, the local police and fire departments got most of his prized teddy bear collection (for children who need comfort), Aaron got his favorite Christmas sweater, certain friends got specific pieces of sculpture, etc. I did much, if not most, of what he wanted me to do.

There is not a weed pot of any description on the mantle or beside the hearth, waiting to be knocked over by playful cats or inadvertently careless people like me.

Tony's been nurturing my cherished Japanese Lace Maple in the yard for four years now. The first year he was under there, his bone ash had so much alkaline in it that it turned the fabulous maroon leaves green (a major disappointment to me, despite the fact that green was his favorite color). I had to wait almost a full year to have them naturally return to the color that pleased me best. It was the only hint I had that he might not be completely thrilled with my final decision, but even that was an ironically sweet thing, not a sad one.

And whether he'd be inclined to admit it or not, I would not be surprised to know that a part of Tony is happy to be in semi-residence there, hanging out with the Japanese Lace Maple, watching my world move by and being entirely at peace with all of it.

Contentedly Ever After

A YEAR OR SO BEFORE Tony's cancer was diagnosed, a time that seems like eons ago, I wrote a short story called "The Fifty-Dollar Marriage." It takes the reader into the thought processes and stray memories of a woman who lives through what appears to be typical day in her life. She's been joyfully married to a great guy for ten years; she is unaware that this is the final day of their marriage and their life together, since the husband dies of a massive coronary that afternoon.

I don't exactly remember the specifics of what motivated me to write the thing in the first place; that's not important here. I will tell you that, like most hopeful romantics, I'm a sucker for happy endings. I am, at the same time, the last person in the world that you want to hand a straight line to; I have been known to put myself in all kinds of personal and professional jeopardy for the sake of a positively stellar punch-line.

This particular tale had one, courtesy of Tony, from the start. I wrote the story from end to beginning, because the punch-line's payoff was undeniably stunning, if not entirely *happy*. It was a tradeoff I was able to make then, with no discernable twinge of conscience.

This was the first of my stories to tiptoe past the concept of death; by the time I'd written it, I'd lost my grandfather, my favorite cousin, an uncle and my father. But up until I began the work on "The Fifty-Dollar Marriage," death hadn't been all that interesting to me in terms of my sense of creative fiction. In those days I'd presumed vaguely that death was just another part of life, and I had dutifully carried around in my head all the canned-response, trite buzz words I'd been taught to associate with loss. Death hadn't reached out a cold fist and slapped me blind yet, so I was able to view it with a benign eye from a safe and utterly naïve distance. I found that I was far more focused on the general notion of loss and the need for hope than I was about the process itself (which was why I had benevolently opted for a clean, fast death for the husband, to get him neatly out of the way so I could tell the part of the story that mattered to me).

I won't tell you much about the story. You can read it yourself one of these days if you want to. I don't mind telling you, though, that it's a good piece of fiction, fun to read. But that's not what's at issue here, and it's not why I'm thinking about that story at the moment.

Here's the thing: when I wrote it, cancer wasn't yet part of our lives. Tony was healthy in those days; our marriage was a happy one. Death was a thing meant for anybody else (preferably as far away from us as possible). It could keep stealthily swimming around other people out there in the darkness if it wanted to. I saw death as more of a useful metaphor than a potentially unwelcome and maddeningly perpetual houseguest.

Over the years, like most everyone else in the world, I had experienced the shock of loss, the pain of dealing with the passage, and the desperate sense of forever missing the person who had been taken away. Still I had always had a protective shield solidly poised between me and the day to day reality of being separated from someone I deeply loved. I didn't realize how long I'd been lucky, until Tony's illness changed the way I looked at most things.

For no particular reason, I happened to look at "The Fifty-Dollar Marriage" the other day. What struck me was that after the staggering loss of her husband, the new widow goes through some interesting mental and emotional gymnastics as she fully begins to experience her pain, rage and fear. I couldn't tell you how or why I knew *precisely* how the new widow felt; I had never personally encountered the depths of unbridled grief before. Yet, I had somehow hit the mark, accurately describing the shock, the disbelief, the strangling sense of helplessness. I had connected with and articulated the paralyzing numbness that seeps like slow poison into every waking moment, which to this day is the thing that continually fascinates me about dealing with the death of our loved ones. I instinctively grasped the blank disconnects and surreal quality a widow's life takes on as she attempts to comprehend for the fiftieth time in the space of a day that she's never going to be able to look into those precious, cherished eyes ever again…

One of the byproducts of writing that story was that for the very first time in my life, I had to come to terms with the harsh, way-too-grown-up idea that there is no such thing as a happy ending in whatever Real Life is. This irks me even as I admit it to you. I know that we can taste and savor happiness throughout our lives; I've done it. But as far as classic Hollywood Happy-Ever-After endings go, there's no such animal. Sorry about that; I'm as disappointed as you are.

I can remember that I scared myself as I wrote that story. Where was the emotional energy behind the words coming from? How could I know these things? I have always had a healthy (and largely hyperactive) imagination, and while I liked the fact that the story itself and the emotion behind it felt real to the people who subsequently read it, I worried about what I was tapping into. I didn't want to know these things; I didn't want to be responsible for them. Without warning, I found myself choking on the realization that no one, including me, was really going to live happily ever after. I had never considered this before.

And in the natural progression of off-the-wall thinking, once I realized that there was no happy ending in store, all I could think about was the ultimate ending, and how death was the end of every story, whether it was written to be that way or not.

As usual, I'd managed to think myself into a corner, and (also as usual) couldn't get out of it alone. I went looking for my husband. He was working on a piece of sculpture in his studio.

I sat down and mumbled my aching discovery to Tony; I had tasted the too-vivid, too-deep sense of the many shades of grief that my character was struggling with. I didn't like the way it made me feel, even second-hand.

I could always tell him anything, and he could generally make me feel better. He listened quietly as I told him how peculiar it felt to be so connected to an intense depth of grief I had never personally experienced.

"Could be that you're remembering how it was from a previous life," Tony said reasonably, with a wry smile. "Or that you're just very tuned in to emotion floating out in the ether. Either way, it's a damned good story." He eyed me speculatively. "What is it that you're *really* worried about?"

It took me a couple of lame attempts before I managed to tell him. I was thinking about death separating us some day, in the remote outposts of the unfathomable distant future, and I was suddenly focused on that separation. Would I be expected to bravely endure the devastating loss of my sweet Tony somehow, just like the poor, sad, numb woman in my story? I'd known that he and I would die at some point, but that knowing was merely a fleeting thought, not bordered by substance; it was the stuff of hypothetical conversation.

Tony did not tease me for obsessing, although he could have. Instead, he hugged me, and said helpfully, "You worry about the damnedest things. Of course we're going to die, some day. And we're going to feel what we feel. There's no getting around it, but there's also no point in resigning yourself to dealing with it all *today*, unless you have nothing else to fret about." He gave me a kiss and chuckled. "But you know, if you could come up with a way for human beings to completely sidestep death and grief, well, *that* would be a story."

Tony was right. If I ever write that story, I'll let you know.

Looking at "The Fifty-Dollar Marriage" now, I have to ask myself honestly: when I wrote it, was I just being glib, as is my habit? Was I simply lucky to hit on it, or was I tapped into something Real? The answer is that I just don't know.

All I can say for certain is that I can truly measure my own pain and grief over Tony's death against my fictional character's grieving experience and emotions. Perched a bit higher above the landscape than I was when I originally wrote the story, from my more experienced view I can see that I indeed hit the sad nail on its horrible little head with an eerie accuracy. And it makes me wonder. What did I really tap into? Is the understanding and wisdom and the ability to cope floating around us somehow? How do we know? And, do we really *want* to know?

But that's not what I meant to tell you.

What I meant to tell you is that despite my stubborn need for happy endings in a slick, storybook world that pretends to promise them to us, I have begun to come to terms with the notion that I actually can live without them. Maybe. (I still catch myself whimpering every so often because there's a part of me that needs happy endings to be true and real somehow, despite the fact that I know better.)

It's taken me a while to be okay with that, but I'm getting there, since I'm expecting so much less than I used to. Instead of looking for happy endings, I'm on the lookout for something a little less spectacular. I've been thinking that perhaps once you sidle up to the idea of genuine contentment—and I absolutely believe that contentment is possible, even after terrible loss—your perspective can shift into a place where you can allow gentle, consistent contentment into your world on a daily basis.

No, I don't believe in the salvation of happy endings any longer, much as I like it when I meet up with them in fiction. I can't expect them in real life again, having traveled long and hard with Tony (who also believed in the sanctity and hope of happy endings). If he were here today, perhaps he could tell me that from his vantage point, his own ending was indeed happy; of course I don't have a way to gauge it or come close enough to possibly understand that.

"Happily ever after" only makes sense to me now in the very short term, which entirely negates the energy behind the "ever-after" part. And even then I'm not so sure about it.

For all my whining about the loss of the cherished absolute of happy endings, I'm a bit more modest these days, if you can believe that. I'm keeping my options open for a small, sweet taste of happiness in my days, a drowsy deliciousness in my nights, and just enough show-stopping punch-lines in between them to make the journey onward worth my while.

I'm all for cutting the ties I seem to have always had to the imaginary, fairytale extremes. It's not a benchmark I can afford any longer.

I think I'm ready to allow myself to learn to live Contentedly Ever After.

Wrangling the Sick Guy

I DON'T GET MUCH CREDIT for my role as Head Tony-Wrangler during the last year of his life, but I really ought to get credit, lots of it, for Wrangling the Sick Guy as often and as well as I did. What's more, I even made it look easy most of the time. As his illness took more of his time and energy, he rebelled in very Tonyish passive-aggressive ways that sometimes could be more challenging than the cancer. Often I ended up having to wrangle our friends along with Tony, an activity which may have added to anyone *else's* idea of fun. I myself saw the necessity of wrangling as yet another thing that had to be done for the Good of the Order. As circumstantially bossy as I have been known to be, I never really wanted to be anyone's Wrangler in the first place.

Tony got to the point where I had to support his need to be commanded to sit down and rest, and put his feet up (we were fighting edema—and losing—but I didn't understand that yet). I also had to order him to eat, nap, and stay down for a short time every day. With the devious style of an overly-precocious four-year-old, Tony managed to find loosely legitimate reasons for getting up, walking around, and getting into trouble. Often he'd wait until we had company; he'd stubbornly rise from the couch and meander through the house looking for his latest drawing or a new book he'd bought. Predictably he'd run out of steam before he got all the way through his search, and he'd wind up standing wherever the energy had faded; he'd talk from that vantage point until he felt stronger and could move on. I ended up hearing from friends later: "He was so tired, why didn't you get up and get what he wanted to show me?"

Conversely (or is that *per*versely?) if I successfully convinced him to stay on the couch for a while with his feet up, and I got him to let me be the one to go and get whatever it was that he wanted to show to someone, he'd make sure it was in a place where I couldn't possibly find it. I'd have to go hunting for it, digging through his desk drawers or scanning his bookshelves or performing a full search and rescue in the garage. He'd get impatient that I couldn't find the thing he wanted. He would finally struggle up off the couch, with the friend generally in tow, and walk precisely to where the thing was sitting (make that hiding). For his finale, he would look at me with a benevolent gaze of tragic sympathy, and nod as he quietly told the friend that I was slowly going senile so he had to do *everything* around the house these days. Later the friend would invariably corner me and ask me in private, "Why don't you let him just get up when he needs to find things? You made him wait while you went looking in all the wrong places. Weren't you listening to him? Are you losing it?"

I heard this from so many people that I added ginko biloba to my diet just to make sure Tony wasn't right about the senility.

I decided early on that even your most caring friends can be terrible Wranglers.

The fight to keep Tony resting regularly throughout the day finally came to a head the first time he fell. I was in the kitchen washing dishes; he was in the bedroom looking for something in his nightstand. I heard a heavy thud, followed by a heavier silence. Hands dripping soap bubbles, I ran to the bedroom.

He was on the floor beside the nightstand. A quick scan showed me that he probably wasn't hurt badly; he had fallen hard but he wasn't bleeding from anywhere that I could see.

When our eyes met, I saw something else: he was madder than hell. At me.

"Why did you do that?" he fumed, danger potent in his voice.

What?

He looked at me with a rage that was so unlike him that it might have been funny in any other situation.

"What made you do that???" demanded my husband as he glared up at me.

"Do what?" I asked, trying unsuccessfully to anticipate him. "What do you think I did?"

Still sitting on the floor, he narrowed his eyes and said very distinctly, "What made you knock me down? What's wrong with you???"

I am not often speechless, but I was then. Uncertain about how to handle this episode, I considered my options carefully, and then went for the one that sounded most like me and also covered this new development accurately. "Are you completely out of your mind?" I couldn't meet the bitterness in his eyes so I looked him over again more carefully and asked in my best, affected Nightingale voice, "So, are you hurt?"

His voice was deep with threat. "No. I am *appalled*."

I couldn't help it. I pressed my lips together tightly so I wouldn't laugh. His dignity, however sketchy, was at issue here, and I did not want to blow it. But he was so cure, and it really was kind of funny. "Does anything hurt?" I asked lightly, trying not to giggle.

"My butt, and my hip," he informed me crossly.

"Well, Honey, it sounded like you fell hard," I said reassuringly, slowly helping him up without letting him put too much of his weight on me. By this time, the cancer, which primarily resided in his belly, weighed upwards of eighty pounds. Roberta had warned me that in the event that Tony fell, I should not try to catch him or break his fall, regardless of what instinct might drive me to do. If my back was ruined, I would be useless to both of us.

By being well out of my reach at the other end of the house, Tony had inadvertently spared me this time.

"I can't believe you'd push me down," he snapped irritably.

"Good. Because I didn't. I was in the kitchen." I showed him my still-soapy hands.

"Then how did I get on the floor?" he demanded, waiting to catch me in a lie.

"You seem to have hit it on your own, Hon," I said. "And loudly, too."

He was not going for it; how could he? Falling was something that frail and fragile elderly people did, not Tony. "Next time," he promised with a wary frown, "I'm going to hit you back."

"You do that," I told him sweetly as together we moved slowly out of the bedroom and back to the couch. After that, he was more in favor of resting for part of every day.

Tony only fell another time or two that I know of. I was not in the vicinity when he did, so we didn't have to address the "knocking to the floor and hitting back" issue. I wonder what I would have done, though. Throughout our years together, while I can admit that I had occasionally made him angry enough to hit me, he never once did. It would never have occurred to him to do so. Instead, one time he beat the hell out of a kitchen chair (and killed it all the way dead). Another time he throttled the very life out of the vacuum cleaner when he would have gotten so much more satisfaction from throttling me. Tony had a very long fuse; whenever he was finally pushed too far (by his wife, or by some of life's more unmanageable circumstances) he lashed out in his art, drawing with a vengeance or shoving clay around in a blinding fury. He never put a hand on me that wasn't gentle.

If he'd fallen and I was close by, would his rage and confusion have allowed him to hit me? What would he have done after that? It's all quiet conjecture now, but I'm fairly certain he'd never have smacked me. Wanted to? Sure. Acted on it? Probably not.

Besides, he knew I had one hell of a right hook.

Tony became obsessed with energy-saving devices the summer before he died. In very little time, he also had our friends caught up in the obsession, showing them his drawings for all kinds of things to make his life easier once he "slowed down." He collected feedback from everyone, painstakingly made modifications to his designs, and spent time perfecting his changes on paper.

He waved a weight-and-pulley-looking drawing at me over lunch one day. "What on earth is that?" I asked, not at all convinced that I really wanted to know.

"This," he said proudly, "is the thing that will keep me mobile when I'm eventually stuck in bed." He showed me (theoretically) how it worked. "See? Here's me, lying in the bed. If I want to get a book, but I can't get up, I can push this lever over here, and this arm will come out, reach across the room and take the book from the dresser and then I can reel it in, and have the book!"

It was all too Rube Goldberg for me; I am made of simpler stuff. "Why don't you just leave the book on your nightstand, so you just have to lean over and pick it up?" I asked.

"You are no fun at all," he grumbled amiably.

There were drawings of inventions for helping him move through the house (something to do with saw-horses that I can't remember now). He came up inventions for bathroom and shower issues ("But can't you just put a stool in the tub and sit there and take your shower?" "Shut up, Lisa."). There were even inventions to help him turn over in bed on his own more easily (he couldn't stay flat in one position for too long because of the uncomfortable weight of the cancer pressing against internal organs). He loved thinking about these new Tony-facilitating devices, loved designing them, and loved talking about them endlessly. Our friends were glad that he was so excited about the inventions, and that kept the conversations lively.

I wisely went out and bought myself a Walkman cassette tape player, which got a great deal of use when what became known as "The Device Drawings" were brought out of Tony's office.

Melissa had to do a lot of Tony-wrangling in those last months. She probably had more of it to do than I did, since she had him consistently during daylight hours on those Tuesdays and Thursdays when I was at work.

She worried when he tried to make his way to the garage (which stands in the back yard, well behind the house). It is not a far walk unless you're carrying heavy cancer around with you. He'd get almost to the garage, and run out of steam, gasping for air. Or he'd suddenly lose his balance, his face white and his hands trembling just enough to scare her. Melissa would convince him that whatever was in the garage that he'd wanted would be easy enough for her to retrieve, and then she'd help him back to the house. Once there, she would con him into lying on the couch and putting his feet up, and could often get him to drink some water or eat lunch after his increasingly common "almost-made-it-to-the-garage" adventures.

Melissa had a clear sense of what he could manage on his own and what he needed help with; she was subtle about getting him to move along to her way of thinking, thus sparing him embarrassment and discomfort, or even danger. At my order, once Tony was determined to put his table saw to good use, Melissa came up with dozens of clever and Tony-friendly distractions and excuses to keep him from using it. She was gentle and easy with him.

Being cast in the juicy role of Queen of the Tyrants opposite Tony's stance as Self-effacing Hero was fine with me; it fit my disposition well. He got off easy having Melissa nix his use of that power saw; I didn't have to be gentle and clever, only very direct.

In a surge of irritable frustration I would have just cut the saw's electrical cord with my scary kitchen scissors and then blithely faced the music.

One day Melissa came out of the bathroom and found Tony sprawled on his hands and knees in the middle of the living room floor, surrounded by and focused on dozens of pictures that he'd scattered from one of his art files. "Check this out, Melissa," he said as he lifted one show her. "Isn't it great that— "

She noticed that he was swaying and breathing heavily, paying far more attention to the art than to his oxygen intake. She had to get him up off the floor. "Are you crazy?" Melissa shouted at him, her voice raised in horrified alarm. "Do you see where you are? Do you know what time it is? Lisa will be home any minute, and if she catches you on the floor and you're not breathing well…for the love of God, Tony, get up, or she'll *kill* you!"

The drama in the voice of the otherwise calm and cool Melissa was interesting enough to pull his attention; he allowed her to help him up. She got him situated at the dining room table and sat down beside him just as I strolled in the front door.

"Hi Guys," I greeted them cheerfully as I came into the room. "What's up?"

"We're just looking at pictures," Tony replied meekly, winking conspiratorially at Melissa, who didn't let him see that she was nodding conspiratorially at *me*.

Melissa was without a doubt the very best Wrangler of the Sick Guy.

Our good friend Jay came to the house one afternoon to hang out with Tony while I went shopping. By that time, I hadn't been out of the house for a couple of weeks, and desperately needed the break from wrangling. The guys knew that I would be gone for the entire afternoon.

Jay had brought with him one of his own favorite films, *Serial Mom*. He had convinced Tony that he would like the film, and they ate lunch and watched the movie together. By all accounts, they had a good time that day.

No, that's something of an understatement: they had a *blast*. How do I know? I know because when I came home from my restful, happy solitary shopping trip some five hours later, both Tony and Jay were, in a word, plastered.

"Lisa," Jay commended me happily, "you have some really good Scotch here!"

Well, I had *had* some good Scotch there, some truly excellent Scotch. It was mostly gone, having been enthusiastically consumed by both Jay and Tony. I was the resident Scotch-drinker in the family, and was very particular about its dispensation. I was not happy. I wanted to scream. And I did, for all the good it did me.

The guys were laughing heartily and agreeing with each other about things I couldn't quite catch, chattering about *Serial Mom*. They all but forgot that I was standing there.

I was livid. The Wrangler of the Day (that would be Jay) had failed to wrangle Tony safely, even after I had given them both very clear directions before I'd left them. It infuriated me that Jay was drunk enough to not be able to help Tony if he had needed it. I was frightened and fuming that Tony had mixed alcohol with his daily rations of Schedule II medication. It was too much for me that between them they'd fed Tony alcohol when he had the stomach capacity of less than half a cup, and was already not getting enough oxygen and blood flow to his brain. He could have fallen. He could have gone into a coma. He could have gotten very sick. He could have died.

In this moment, I was prepared to kill him myself. And I was willing to throw Jay into the bargain.

I was out of my mind with blistering rage. Eventually recognizing the danger in my eyes, Tony fumbled to stand up from his cozy position on the couch. "Sit down!" I commanded. He dropped like a big sack of late-autumn apples.

Next I focused my hurricane pointedly on Jay; I swore and screeched and threatened, until I realized in mid-roar that he was smiling at me beatifically, proud of a job well done.

They were impossible; I glared evilly at each of them in turn, and when that had no effect on them, I glowered at them together. Undaunted, they grinned back at me. Tony may even have waved.

Jay was cheery enough under the influence to recognize that I was miffed, but was in no condition to be too worried about my ranting. I sighed and gave up. What else could I do? And as I settled down I realized for the first time that Tony was, in this drunken, hazy hour, more relaxed, peaceful and yeah, happier than he'd been in literal months.

Still seething, I called Roberta and told her what I'd come home to. Was Tony in any real danger? Not as long as he didn't fall down, Roberta advised with a chuckle. Would he be sick later from the alcohol? Maybe, Roberta said, but that was something I was used to dealing with; Tony's system was growing ever more fragile, and food as often as not disagreed with him. She told me to calm down, to help Jay to sober up, and to put Tony to bed. She didn't join me in my righteous fury. She was no help at all.

So I made really bad hot tea for Jay, got him to eat something, and spent the next hour letting him take a nap in the chair across from the couch on which Tony was now snoring happily, my favorite single-malt whisky coursing merrily through his veins and sweetening his sleep.

Later, when Jay was completely able to drive, I sent him on his way. "Am I in trouble?" he asked a little sheepishly.

"You bet," I said as peevishly as I could manage around a smile. He walked to his truck and got in, glancing back at me uncertainly since he knew I was about to call my friend Donna, who is married to Jay.

I only told her that Jay was on his way home, and that I had been the cause of his delay. I don't know whether she heard the irritation or the chuckle in my voice, but she knew there was something going on. "Is everything okay?" she asked carefully.

"Yeah. Jay will tell you all about it when he gets home."

I do not know what happened to Jay when Donna found out what had occurred at my house with *Serial Mom* and the Scotch, but I don't think it was especially pretty. Donna has an unerring sense of what is okay and what is not, and she knows how to deal with stuff that falls into the Not Okay category. Tough as I am, I would not have liked being Jay when he got home to Donna that evening.

For his part, Tony was mostly all right despite his dip into too much of my Scotch. He did apologize later for the amount that they had ingested, but by that time I was so entertained at the picture of the two of them loaded in the living room that I couldn't get or stay mad. And when Jay and Donna and I talk about the episode now, it's with much affection. The boys were so damned cute, laughing about the movie and the time they'd spent talking and drinking together. It's become one of my favorite memories of that last month that Tony was with me.

Was Jay a good Wrangler of the Sick Guy? I wanted to bellow a resounding NO that day, but the way things have worked out, I'm not so sure that's the right answer.

It was a bad day for the Head Wrangler. I was unsuccessfully trying to overcome my very reasonable fear of the scary motorized weed-destroyer that Tony had bought a couple of years before, the thing he liked best when we did yard work. It was noisy, it was a little heavier than I wanted to deal with, and it had some very sharp and dangerous things going on at its business end. I had visions of blades of grass screaming in its wake, blended with images of bloody sneakers whenever Tony walked the damned thing around the back yard.

I hated it.

I hated it even more when it became obvious to us that Tony would no longer be handling the yard work. I was going to be the Lawn Maven, and I was cranky as hell about it. I did not want to pick up one more chore that Tony had had to drop, but there was no help for it. To compensate, I bitched. Loudly.

Tony was not altogether sympathetic, nor was he overly helpful. "What's the problem?" he asked impatiently from the other side of the sliding screen door in the dining room. I sat on the patio step and whined about the inherent evils of the weed-destroyer and its noisy motor and how much I did not want to learn to use it.

He was not moved. "All you have to do is start it by pulling on the cord, then throttling for a minute, then turn the knob over there, and then go get the weeds. Nothing could be easier."

I growled at him, but he ignored me, and sat down at the table so he could watch me. "Not that one, the *other* one. That's the throttle.

Now pull the cord to start the engine."

I pulled. Nothing happened. I pulled again. Nothing happened again.

Tony groaned in frustration. "Why don't I just change my clothes and come out there and—"

"Yeah, right," I snapped. "You'll last long enough to get out here, and then you'll be too tired to do anything but sit around and tell me what I'm doing wrong, which, by the way, you're already doing. No thanks!"

He was more frustrated about having to surrender one more of his responsibilities to his waning strength and failing body than he was irritated with me. I was more upset that he was one step closer to losing his dignity along with his fight than I was that I had to deal with the satanic weed-cutter. In his frustration and my upset, we barked at each other, the sniping all out of proportion to the stupid yard work.

While he didn't actually insult my intelligence, he did imply that not only was I not mechanically gifted, but also I didn't seem to have the basic motor skills to start a…motor. While I didn't entirely blame him for increasingly dumping one more strenuous and time-consuming job on me, I inferred that he'd never been big on getting his chores done anyway, and that his being sick was just a snazzy way of avoiding the yard work, the litter boxes and anything else that he hadn't ever been wild about doing around the house.

He roared at me; I, ever the wildcat when riled, hissed and spat back at him. I slammed the weed-destroyer against the patio step and he slammed himself away from the dining room table and went to bed, threatening icily to find a way to have the weed-destroyer come after *me*.

I was furious. I wanted to have him shot. No, I wanted to shoot him myself, to make sure the job got done right.

I sat on the patio step for a very long time and, feeling more than a little murderous, considered my options.

After I calmed down, I called Roberta.

"Hi, what's going on?" she asked cheerfully. I was still mad at Tony, the Tony she thought was so wonderful and perfect. I sneered at her naïveté; the wicked side of my nature was running the show, and I liked it that way. "I have a question for you."

"Shoot," Roberta said. She is a perceptive woman, more on the money this time than she realized.

"I wanted to know something." I took a breath. "When the death is expected, like Tony's will be, do they automatically do autopsies?"

Roberta thought for a moment, slowed only by the note of genuine inquisitiveness in my voice. "Not usually, no. Why?"

"That's good," I said craftily. "If that's the case, do you think anyone will notice when Tony's dead that there's a bright red garden trowel sticking out of his big, stupid head?"

"Lisa!" Roberta gasped. Then she started to laugh. "I take it he's making you a little crazy today?"

I told her what had happened between us, and she listened with enough sympathy to make me feel a little less like a spoiled child, and a little more like a tired, anxious-to-avoid-the-future wife. She understood what Tony and I were really battling over, and pointed out that it sounded like we were fighting on the same side, despite our coming at the issue from entirely different directions.

So I learned one more lesson about the fine art of wrangling that day: that wrangling, the hands-on and sometimes heart-on herding of and caring for the one you love, happens in many different (and sometimes unexpected) ways that don't always make sense to anyone but of the two of you.

Our last fight was one of those unexpected wrangling efforts. I admit I was not at my best, but I did what I thought I had to do in the circumstances. It is why you can never trust me to take the high road.

Two weeks before he died, he wanted to watch a movie that I didn't have any interest in. He wanted me to watch it with him. I wrinkled my nose at him, but he prodded until I gave in.

I didn't like the movie, couldn't follow the plotline because I wasn't in the mood to be patient with it. He saw that I didn't like the film, and he was bothered by this (Tony was always very proud of his uncanny ability to gauge things that would please me, and he was most often right; but not this time, at least not right away.)

"Stick with it, you'll like this film in a little while. Give the exposition time," he suggested, and I rolled my eyes at him in abject boredom.

I still didn't like the film ten minutes later, but by that time I wasn't thinking about the film. Something was wrong with Tony. He was sitting in his chair, eyes on the television, calmly and patiently doing some focused relaxation exercise he'd learned in his Qi Gong classes eight months before.

"What's wrong?" I asked quickly, my voice immediately tense and high.

"Oh, I don't know," he said blandly. "Just watch the film. The exercise will take care of it."

I took a breath. Tony was a master of understatement, and had a horror of making a scene, even when a scene was absolutely required. I sat on the couch and watched him focus on his calm breathing, and stared at him as he moved his hands delicately over his cancer-round belly. I noticed that his face was looking a little grayer than usual.

"What is wrong???" I pressed. "What's happening? What do you need?"

He looked at me and said softly "I need you to watch the damned movie."

Too often in the past months, Tony's unwillingness to tell me what was happening with him had backfired and caused us close calls too many times. He was not good at speaking up when he was in trouble. Yes, he believed in the efficacy of his Qi Gong practice, and so did I, to a fine point; it soothed him, it helped him to focus and get grounded, and opened him up to deep meditation. All good things, but unfortunately no substitute for the Emergency Room.

"What's going on with you?" I demanded. "Does something hurt?"

"Yes," he said through clenched teeth. "But it will not hurt quite so much if you just watch the movie and leave me alone." He focused on his Qi Gong movement and pulled his consciousness inward.

The Head Wrangler lost it. There was no style, no flair, no elegance to my technique here. Months, maybe years, of anxiety and fear coated with rage and panic bubbled up in me in that instant. I thoroughly, and with feeling, lost all trace of the thinly-protective sheen of composure that I was used to hiding behind.

I thundered and rained on him, shaking with the cold of my own terror and fury. I gave him hell about not telling me what was really happening with him. I screeched at him for staying distant and emotionally unavailable throughout the long years of his illness. I blamed him for keeping me out in the dark instead of letting me know what he was feeling so that we could share our information and cope better with the nasty circumstances we faced. Most of my tirade was entirely wasted, lost on Mr. Selective Hearing; the only thing he felt in the mighty downpour was my never-before-disclosed contempt for his Qi Gong. This wounded him deeply enough to make him hurl a little lightning of his own.

He told me angrily that I'd never been supportive of his Qi Gong, which both upset and offended him deeply, since he felt it was the best coping tool that he had at his disposal. He yelled that I'd never appreciated his practice, and had not been willing to join him in it, and that I had thus been disloyal and unsupportive of his process, which he found disheartening and made him feel like he was fighting his battle all alone.

It did not help that I hissed back that I thought I had been supportive enough to *pay* for the blasted Qi Gong classes, but we were both well past any semblance of reasonability at that point.

He looked terrible, felt like hell, and pulled himself out of his Qi Gong. He reached for the television remote, and turned the movie off with a snarl so weak that my heart nearly stopped. He sat back in the chair, closed his eyes, and tried to breathe steadily, but failed as he began to cry in front of me for only the second time since the cancer had been diagnosed, ten years earlier.

The sight undid me; still I recognized at once that crying was probably the best thing for him. I hurried to him, and dropped to my knees in front of his chair, putting my arms around him as gently as I could, as firmly as I dared.

"You never thought Qi Gong would help me," he sobbed. "It's kept me calm, it's kept me focused, it's kept me from having to really look at the cancer. It *has* helped! And you're so negative about it!"

I found myself making those mindless, lame soothing noises that I swore I'd never make to anyone. I stroked his hair. He didn't settle down; he was on a roll, one he had earned and richly deserved. He was more than entitled to it.

"Qi Gong is all about life! It keeps me from thinking about death, Lisa. I don't want to die!" he sobbed wretchedly, his shoulders convulsing as he wound himself up instead of down. "I *don't* want to die! But there's nothing I can do about it! I'm going to die, and I'm scared and I'm tired and I feel like shit and there's nothing I can do about any of it!"

Now he was unable to catch his breath for the weeping. His color had changed subtly from gray to pink to faintly blue. I was going to have to do or say something to rein him back in. But I didn't have a clue what that was; telling him to stop crying wasn't it. Neither was telling him that everything was going to be all right; we already knew that it wasn't. What was I going to do? What could I possibly say to him?

The Head Wrangler was about to fail Tony in a big way.

He was gasping for air, so overcome with the range of emotions he'd suppressed for so long that he couldn't stop talking as he cried. "I don't want to leave, I don't want to leave you, and I'm going to anyway, no matter how much I want to stay with you! I'm dying, I'm really dying, and dying is so hard! Can you understand? Dying is hard!"

And in that instant he gave me the handle I needed so I could save him. It was perfect, it was priceless, and I knew in a heartbeat that it could go either way.

Naturally, I went for it.

I moved a little away from him, so he could see my face clearly. "No, I think you've got it wrong, Love," I murmured softly enough to pull his focus.

"What?"

"You've got it wrong."

The sobbing quieted slightly as he tried to listen.

"Got what wrong?"

"You've got it wrong. You said: 'Dying is hard.' But I think you've got it wrong. You are descended from a long line of actors;

you should know this. I think you meant 'Dying is *easy*. *Comedy* is hard.'" I glued my eyes to his, and breathed a desperate prayer for assistance to the glowing memory of the great actor Edmund Keane, who'd spent his dying theatrical breath uttering these famous last words.

As my remark stood frozen in the air between us, I watched as Tony's face fractionally moved from grief and pain to a kind of stunned shock. I held my breath.

And then it happened.

The left corner of his mouth began to twitch ever so slightly upward as he mentally played back the words I'd spoken. His tears slowed and then stopped as the right side of his mouth twitched faintly, too, the forming smile unsteady but building momentum. The sound he made wasn't as much a laugh as it was a gasp of genuine relief.

In a rush I let go of the breath I was holding, and rearranged my face to give him a tartly smug look of *"Ta-DAH! So—what are you going to say about* ***that****?"* at which Tony, an actor all the way down to the bone, began to chuckle. He couldn't help it.

I threw my arms around him then, and we laughed hysterically, holding each other as the giggles carried us out of despair and back into the safety of a far less oppressive space.

A half-hour later he decided that whatever pain had been threatening him had dissipated into manageability (with the help of whatever clever combination of drugs I searched through and insisted that he take). Despite the fact that we were both still giggling (at my timing, my memory, my glib audacity, his delighted shock at it and my relief that I had momentarily saved the day) he really wanted to finish watching the damned movie.

I stared at the TV with one part of my brain, and reflected on the evening's experience with another. What was wrong with me? How could I have had the balls to say what I'd said to him? *I couldn't even let him cry*, I screeched at myself. Had I been truly respectful of his process? Did the happier, less awful end result justify what I had done and said to him?

Covertly studying him as he sat in his favorite chair and watched the film, I could see that he was feeling all kinds of better. I decided that agonizing over my methods was a waste of time that we just didn't have.

Sometimes wrangling isn't as easy as it looks from the outside; all that can matter is that you get the job done and done well enough to get by, at least until next time.

But that's not what I meant to tell you.

What I meant to tell you is that I never wanted to be a Wrangler, not of sick guys, not of anyone. These days I barely manage to summon up the energy to wrangle the cats who own me. It's not because I'm not capable of it, it's because I don't want to.

I remember telling Tony early in our relationship that I had never been a person who nagged anyone at all until I was with *him*; it was his fault that I was a nag of a wife because living with him had surely made me one. He didn't buy it for a minute, and when I'm honest, neither did I (but it was a good story and I stuck to it, for years).

All right, so I wasn't a bad Wrangler, not ever. I'm just bossy enough to have a good handle on the skill set required to be an exceptional Wrangler (and I'd make a pretty decent Empress as well, but that's a conversation for another time). It's that I didn't want to be put in a position to have to be a Wrangler for the—for *my*—Sick Guy. I didn't want to have to deal with the fact that he was very ill and was going to die; I didn't want him to be sick in the first place. Like everyone else in the world I simply wanted our life to be what I wanted it to be, the way I'd planned for it to be, at least in terms of the big stuff.

Tough, said the Universe calmly.

Dammit, I seethed back. This is just not fair.

I'd already learned the nasty truth long ago: Fair is Fiction. Dammit.

So I Wrangled the Sick Guy as often as I thought he needed it, sometimes loudly, overtly and with enough swagger to keep myself together, other times with silent strength of purpose, subtle moves toward holding Tony safe and close while he finished out his cycle.

The thing about Wranglers, I see now, is that even though we think we're working all on our own, solitary in the darkness, we're really part of a team despite our disparate approaches, adventures and attitudes.

Tony needed the Wrangler in me, but he also needed some degree of Wrangler in our friends, especially Melissa and Jay. I needed those Wranglers, too.

And the fact that I continue to survive as well as I do makes me notice without too much surprise that my sweet Tony was most likely doing some Lisa-Wrangling of his own.

The Widow Steps Back and I Move Forward

I DON'T EXPECT THAT YOU'LL believe me when I tell you that I didn't really want to write this book. Oh, don't get me wrong; I've gotten used to the idea, and I hope that you'll be able to relate a lot of what has happened in your progress toward healing to some of the things I've said here. If I can help, I'm glad about that.

When I finally came to grips with the fact that Tony was dying, that the final outcome of the journey was set in stone and I couldn't rescue him from what was surely going to happen to him (and by association, to me), I stopped writing in my journal. I didn't want to record how I felt, what I thought and what I feared most in the first place, and I didn't believe I'd ever want to re-read any of it. Why would I want to put myself through any of this stuff again?

I locked my journal in my desk and ignored it for nearly three years.

With that in mind, it strikes me as slightly strange how, in the process of writing of this book, I find that the memories and late-night terrors that my remembering has unearthed haven't required the pain-streaked words I might have recorded in my journal. Everything I needed in order to recreate each episode recounted here was waiting patiently inside me, taking me back to the actual events, everything eerily intact down to the nuances. The grins I'd forgotten about were right there, along with the tears, the anger, the unrelenting anxiety, the loneliness, and all the fear. My memories gave me back the funny moments as well as the bitter times of utter, irreconcilable defeat. All I had left to do was to go back into the dreaded darkness, and try to make sense of it for myself. I had to actively come to terms with every bit of it.

Hell, it would have been much easier to crib from what I normally would have written in my journal. Perhaps then I wouldn't have had to dig too deeply; I might even have been able to maintain the full force of my self-protective, glib outlook on the way things are. But that wouldn't have helped me much, wouldn't have prepared me to be willing and eventually ready to tell you how it was for Tony and me.

It's a relatively new development in my life, and it's a significant one, I think: recently I've all but stopped using Tony's surname. You won't find it in this book. I'm not denying who I have been as Tony's wife, and, okay, as Tony's widow (I think you already get that). I find that I am ready to move forward without his name as surely as I'm getting used to moving forward without him. We didn't have children and I have no contact with the remaining members of his family; I have no pressing reason to hold on to the name.

He doesn't need the name any longer, either. There is no gravestone marking the spot where his ashes reside. Tony had a strange and sometimes warped idea about touching the planet only ever so lightly with his life, leaving something better than it was when he got here, certainly, but mostly not making a mess. Respecting that, I've gone back to my own name, my pre-Tony name. And I'm good with that. He would be, too.

I've accepted, over the space of the four very long years without him, that I'm finally moving out of my much-celebrated "Tony Phase," although the happy and hard repercussions of the Tony Effect in my life and in the way I choose to continue will be with me, thankfully, until the end of my days.

I marvel at how I've changed since he died; I can count more definitive modifications, alterations, epiphanies and evolutions in the past six years—the last two of his losing battle and the four since then—than perhaps I've seen in my life over the past twenty.

Much as I hate to give his illness credit for generating anything at all positive (hating cancer and what it can do still feeds a fever in me I can't quite cool and be at peace with), I have to admit that I am stronger for having been dragged kicking and screaming through the horrors of the experience. It's possible that because of the journey through our situation, I carry what I believe to be a mostly-healthy perspective on life and death that I could not have acquired any other way. I know what it's like to survive for days and sometimes weeks at a time without taking a steady, deep, nourishing breath. I understand how a person can weep until his or her body suddenly stops in mid-sob because it simply cannot continue to cry like that. I have learned the hard way that a saving dawn comes after even the darkest night; I also own the sorry truth that sometimes the most welcome, wished-for morning light can be as cold, colorless, and distant as the bleak, treacherous, black hours that preceded it.

I believe that I have a greater capacity for compassion now than I did six years ago. I know that I understand more fully the rightness of honoring the process of every person with whom I come into contact.

Am I always compassionate? Do I always remember to make room for and respect everyone's processes?

No, I'm not, and no, I don't, not always. And that's because I also learned throughout the rigors of Tony's illness and death and the painful, usually solitary reconstruction of my life without him that I am, first and foremost, excruciatingly human. I am just as likely to fail at what I know to be the right thing to do as I am to succeed at it.

Am I a sweeter, softer, kinder, nicer or gentler version of myself now than I was before his illness took him away from me? I'd say not, and the people who know me best would most likely agree with me. I was Hell On Wheels before my life with Tony changed, and I'm Hell On Wheels today; it's only that I usually pay more attention to where and how I use my furious and frantic energy. I'm less likely to waste it on things that don't matter.

It's odd to me that I have two cats that Tony doesn't know. It's sobering to accept that I drive a car Tony's never seen, that I shamelessly enjoy a rock-star-caliber bathroom acquired only because Tony died. It startles me sometimes that physically I look very different from the woman Tony loved for so long. As I've moved away from the person I was, and move toward the person I choose to be, I've noticed with a recurring ripple of genuine surprise that much of the external me is markedly different. More than that, the way my mind works has permanently changed. I think it's fair to say that my entire world has shifted dramatically and would be strange to him.

Would he know in a heartbeat that the woman walking on the path toward him after four years (and a seeming lifetime) full of changes was the woman to whom he gave his heart? I wonder if he'd be able to sense and easily identify my essential, internal living energy as surely as I've recognized his after-energy, in passing. I'd like to think so, but as I continue to change, and yes, to age, I wonder if he really could.

But that's not what I meant to tell you.

What I meant to tell you is that, while I never believed in the beginning that I'd ever feel this way, much less come right out and say it, I *do* want a new life, now, since my old one was broken beyond repair. It's not easy to confess, but after writing this book I don't seem to have too many secrets left:

I don't want to be alone with the cats for the next forty years.

Tony taught me about living in love, and I don't think the end result of two decades of the laughter and passion, craziness and frustration and magic I had with him should be wasted, pacing solitarily in some shadowy corridor of memory for the rest of my life.

I know that I will always miss him. I'll always feel the loss of him, and yearn for the laughter we won't share, for the dreams that we had to give up because cancer always got the last word. I'll love him every day for the rest of my life; he will not become an abstraction (although he'd have liked that, the bastard) because he was a fundamental, catalystic, absolute fact of my life. As long as I live, a part of him will live on in and with me.

In my view, that's as it should be: I am much of who I am because I loved Tony, and because I let him love me.

I hope he remembers to check in with me, making Grand Gestures and Encore Performances as I move through the rest of the pages of my life. If I am lucky enough to find love again with someone else, I am secure in the knowledge that Tony wants me to be happy.

A week or so after Tony died, my mother hit me with one of the most desperately bitter statements I have ever heard: "After he's been gone a few years, it will seem like he was never here at all."

Once I caught my breath, the impact of her remark became a glistening key for me, one I could use to unlock a truth I might not have stumbled on for a while, but which I seem to have needed at precisely the second my mother said it. Her comment was predicated on her own experience, not mine. I was grateful that I'd already come to solid terms with my choice to try to honor the processes of other people, and to accept that my take on any given situation is only my take, and doesn't necessarily apply to anyone else's life, and vice versa. Otherwise, I might have been devastated by her words. I was able to see that those words spoke for her; they did not and could not speak for me.

I think about that conversation with her, years later, and I only feel badly for my mother. I'm sorry about the experiences she had that caused her to perceive her own reality in that way.

My marriage, my friendship, and my love affair with Tony were not the kinds of things that could fizzle into nothingness simply because he isn't around any longer to breathe life into them every day. Tony has been here, he has marked me, and I will never forget.

For the record, I do not label myself a widow, even though that's still considered my current legal marital status. I simply accept that I'm "no longer married" and that's good enough for me. I'm a woman whose husband died. I've learned — and continue to learn — many lessons that have their somber origins in my history with Tony's cancer and death. On the other hand, I don't want the experiences that I lived through (and that Tony didn't) to define me or speak for me.

I can finally cop to the fact that there's a genuine part of me that only wanted to write this book so I wouldn't have to tell these damned stories any longer. There was comfort in the belief that I could just say, "Look at Page 18 if you want to know what happened when..."

It's taken me a while to get over myself, but I have come to intimately understand that it is the telling of personal stories from the bright and also the grief-shadowed, darkly bleak hours of our lives that defines who we are. Our stories allow us to connect with others in the sacred face of our precious common humanity, and maybe most importantly, sharing the tales of our journey gives our suffering as well as our survival *meaning*. And I think that, at the end of the day, this is what it's really all about.

No, I don't see myself as a widow any longer. I see myself as a woman trying to give something back, a woman alone, very much alive and ready to play again, albeit without her favorite playmate.

I'm a Work In Progress, an optimistic, hopeful romantic, a more focused and purposeful version of Hell On Wheels.

Am I anxious and frightened? Often. Am I lonely on a scale I don't want to contemplate, much less approach? Sometimes; it depends on what day it is. Do I know what I want? Vaguely. Am I willing to go after whatever that is? Without question, and without hesitation.

I don't know about you, but it looks to me as though I'm very much back in the game. There are a few less cheerleaders than there were before, but I can handle that as I move forward into the healing power of Life as it flows graciously around me and offers me a new day, every day.

I see myself now as someone who, after losing nearly all the love she had and then losing too much of herself in the process, somehow has come full-circle. It's a staggering, mind-blowing miracle to me, but the person I am today has the capacity to give and share more love than she can ever spend. It is an added blessing as well as an absolute certainty that Tony would want nothing less than that for me.

I am a survivor. I have survived a long and terrible journey and a devastating loss. I deserve to be happy and well, and I deserve to find light and love in the world as I continue to move through it.

You deserve it, too.

And that's exactly what I meant to tell you.

The Same Old Sun

by Eric Woolfson and Alan Parsons (from The Alan Parsons Project album *Vulture Culture*)

Tell me what to do
Now the light in my life is gone from me
Is it always the same
Is the night never–ending

Tell me what to do
All the hopes and the dreams went wrong for me
There's a smile on my face
But I'm only pretending

Taking my life
One day at a time
Cause I can't think what else to do
Taking some time
To make up my mind
When there's no one to ask but you

The same old sun would shine in the morning
The same bright eyes would welcome me home
And the moon would rise way over my head
And get through the night alone

And the same old sun will shine in the morning
The same bright stars will welcome me home
And the clouds will rise way over my head
I'll get through the night on my own

Tell me what to do
Now there's nobody watching over me
If I seem to be calm
Well it's all an illusion

Tell me what to do
When the fear of the night comes over me
There's a smile on my face
Just to hide the confusion

Taking my life
One day at a time
Cause I can't think what else to do
Taking some time
To make up my mind
When there's no one to ask but you

The same old sun would shine in the morning
The same bright eyes would welcome me home
And the moon would rise way over my head
I'll get through the night alone

And the same old sun will shine in the morning
The same bright stars will welcome me home
And the clouds will rise way over my head
I'll get through my life on my own

Lisa Courtney is a novelist and poet whose unwitting foray into nonfiction with *Widow's Weeds: Lessons Learned from the Death of a Partner* has not, as she originally feared, pulled her too far away from her comfortably-neurotic literary roots in fantasy and fiction. Widowed in 2001 (and still a little miffed about that), she shares her home in the Pacific Northwest with a nearly-manageable number of cats and a decidedly unmanageable number of books. She is currently at work on her second novel.

ISBN 141208800-3

9 781412 088008